£2.40

D1391741

Mrs Beeton's
Favourite Recipes

Other Concorde Cookery Books

COOKING FOR YOUR FREEZER
PREPARING FOOD FOR YOUR FREEZER

£2.95
NET UK ONLY

Previous page: Hot Savoury Toasts

Mrs Beeton's Favourite Recipes

Edited by
Maggie Black

WARD LOCK LIMITED•LONDON

ACKNOWLEDGEMENTS

The Editor would like to thank all the people and
institutions who have supplied specialist advice,
and the manufacturers who have advised on the
use of modern food products.

ISBN 0 7063 1427 1

First published in Great Britain 1972 by Ward
Lock Limited, 116 Baker Street, London, W1M
2BB, a Pentos Company.

Text in Baskerville (169/312)

Reproduced, printed and bound
in Great Britain by
Fakenham Press Limited,
Fakenham, Norfolk

Introduction

THIS BOOK GIVES YOU the best of the tried, trusted recipes which have brought the name of Mrs Beeton lasting fame. They are all classic dishes, brought up to date by using modern ingredients and suitable quantities for today's smaller families. 'Instant' foods, for example, are part of our scene, and have been included.

This is not a book for complete beginners. When Mrs Beeton wrote, cookery was still taught mostly by word of mouth, recipes were vague and oven heats were temperamental. So she wrote down every detail, word by word. But today we have no such excuses for not knowing how to cook. So the modern editors expect you to know how to boil an egg, make breadcrumbs, whip egg whites and so on.

But no one can remember all the precise cooking times, or the correct proportions of ingredients to use, even of familiar, favourite recipes. Here lies the value of this book. You can look them up whenever you want to make a classic dish, and you cannot go wrong.

Contents

	Page
Weights and Measures	7
Soups and First Courses	10
Soups	10
Hors D'œuvres	13
Breakfast, Brunch and Supper Dishes	18
Sandwiches and Savoury Pastries	23
Fish Dishes	30
Shellfish Dishes	38
Meat Dishes	43
Roasted and Grilled Meats	43
Braised, Boiled and Reheated Meat Dishes	50
Meat Pies and Puddings	58
Offal Dishes	61
Cold Meats	63
Poultry and Game Dishes	67
Vegetable Dishes	83
Vegetable Side Dishes	83
Main Course Vegetable Dishes	89
Salads	91
Puddings, Desserts and Ices	94
Basic Recipes, Sauces and Trimmings	108
Menus	122

Weights and Measures Used in this Book

Liquid measures

60 drops	1 teaspoon
3 teaspoons	1 tablespoon
4 tablespoons	$\frac{1}{2}$ gill
1 gill	$\frac{1}{4}$ pint
4 gills	1 pint
2 pints	1 quart
4 quarts	1 gallon

Homely solid measures

Spoons are British Standard teaspoons and table-spoons, which hold the amounts of liquid given above. They are measured with the contents levelled off, i.e. all the spoonfuls are level spoonfuls.

The cup is a British Standard measuring cup which holds 10 fluid oz or an Imperial $\frac{1}{2}$ pint.

Homely solid measures

Flour, sifted	3 tablespoons	1 oz
Castor or granulated sugar	2 tablespoons	$1\frac{1}{4}$ oz
Icing sugar, sifted	3 tablespoons	1 oz
Butter or margarine	2 tablespoons	$1\frac{1}{4}$ oz
Cornflour	2 tablespoons	1 oz
Granulated or powdered gelatine	4 teaspoons	$\frac{1}{2}$ oz
Golden syrup or treacle	1 tablespoon	1 oz
Flour, sifted	1 cup	5 oz
Castor or granulated sugar	1 cup	9 oz
Icing sugar, sifted	1 cup	5 oz
Butter or margarine	1 cup	9 oz
Cornflour	1 cup	8 oz
Golden syrup or treacle	1 cup	1 lb

Metric measures

It is almost impossible to try to convert British Standard weights into absolutely accurate metric measures. The exact equivalent of one ounce is 28.35 grams and that of one pound is 453.6 grams. When converting recipes that call for fairly small quantities, a unit of 25 grams can be used as the equivalent of 1 ounce, but the larger the quantity, the less accurate the substitution will become. Most scales today are calibrated in grams as well as ounces and more accurate results will be obtained by calculating 28 grams to the ounce. A 15 cm sandwich tin can replace a 6 inch one; and a 20×14 cm tin ($8 \times 5\frac{1}{2}$ inch) will take a Yorkshire pudding using 100 grams of plain flour.

Oven temperatures

	Electric	Celsius	Gas Regulo Mark
Very cool	225 °F	110 °C	$\frac{1}{4}$
Very cool	250 °F	130 °C	$\frac{1}{2}$
Very cool	275 °F	140 °C	1
Cool	300 °F	150 °C	2
Warm	325 °F	170 °C	3
Moderate	350 °F	180 °C	4
Fairly hot	375 °F	190 °C	5
Fairly hot	400 °F	200 °C	6
Hot	425 °F	220 °C	7
Very hot	450 °F	230 °C	8
Very hot	475 °F	240 °C	9

Deep fat frying table

Food	Bread Browns In	Fat Temp	Oil Temp
Uncooked mixtures, e.g. fritters	1 minute	370–375 °F	375–385 °F
Cooked mixtures, e.g. fish cakes	40 seconds	380–385 °F	385 °F
Fish	1 minute	375 °F	375 °F
Potato straws, chips, etc	20 seconds	390 °F	395 °F

9

Soups and First Courses

SOUPS

CONSOMMÉ (basic)

Make and clear stock for consommé. Simmer until the consommé is the strength required.

CONSOMMÉ JULIENNE

1 qt consommé

Garnish

1 tablesp shreds of carrot	1 tablesp finely chopped onion
1 tablesp shreds of turnip	1 tablesp shreds of celery
1 tablesp shreds of green leek	

Cut the shreds $\frac{1}{16}$ in thick and $1-1\frac{1}{4}$ in long. Boil them separately for a few minutes till just tender, then drain them and pour the hot consommé on to them.

6 helpings

CONSOMMÉ ROYALE

1 qt consommé

Royal Custard shapes

2 egg yolks	1 tablesp milk
Salt and pepper	or stock

To make the custard, mix the egg yolks with the seasoning and the milk or stock. Strain it into a small greased basin. Stand the basin in hot water and steam the custard until it is firm. Turn out the custard, cut it into thin slices, and from these cut tiny fancy shapes with a 'brilliant' cutter. Add them to the hot consommé.

6 helpings

FRENCH ONION SOUP

2 oz fat bacon	$\frac{1}{4}$ pt white wine
6 medium-sized onions	or cider
$\frac{1}{2}$ oz flour	6 small slices of bread
Salt and pepper	2 oz cheese:
$\frac{1}{2}$ teasp French mustard	Gruyère or Parmesan
$1\frac{1}{2}$ pt stock	A little butter

Chop the bacon and heat it gently in a deep pan till the fat runs freely. Slice the onions thinly and fry them slowly in the bacon fat till golden. Add the flour, salt and pepper to taste and continue frying for a few minutes. Stir in the mustard, the stock and the wine or cider. Simmer till the onions are quite soft. Toast the bread, grate the cheese. Butter the toast and spread the slices with grated cheese. Pour the soup into individual fireproof soup bowls, float a round of toast on each and brown it in a very hot oven or under the grill.

6 helpings

MINESTRONE

$\frac{1}{4}$ lb haricot beans	1 glass red wine
3 pt water	2 carrots
2 onions	1 small turnip
1–2 cloves of	2 sticks of celery
garlic	2 small potatoes
1 oz lean bacon	$\frac{1}{2}$ small cabbage
scraps	2 oz macaroni
2 tablesp olive	*or* fancy shapes
oil	of Italian pasta
A bunch of herbs	Salt and pepper
2 large tomatoes	Grated cheese

Soak the beans overnight in $\frac{1}{2}$ pt of the water. Slice the onions, crush the garlic, chop the bacon. Heat the oil in a deep pan and fry the onion very gently for 10 min. Add the garlic, bacon, herbs, cut-up tomatoes and the wine. Reduce this mixture by rapid boiling for 5 min. Add the haricot beans and all the water and simmer for 2 hr. Dice the carrots, turnip and celery and add them to the soup; simmer for a further $\frac{1}{2}$ hr. Add the potatoes, diced, and simmer for another $\frac{1}{2}$ hr. Add the shredded cabbage and the macaroni and simmer for a final 10–15 min. Season the soup, stir into it a little grated cheese and hand the rest round separately. Different mixtures of vegetables may be used.

6 helpings

TOMATO SOUP

1 lb tomatoes,	Grated nutmeg
fresh *or* canned	Lemon juice
1 onion	A bunch of herbs
1 carrot	Minute tapioca *or*
$\frac{1}{2}$ oz margarine	cornflour
1 oz bacon scraps,	Salt and pepper
rind *or* bone	Red colouring, if
1 pt white stock	needed
or juice from	
canned tomatoes	

Slice the tomatoes, onion and carrot. If canned tomatoes are used, strain them and make the juice up to 1 pt with stock. Melt the margarine in a deep pan and lightly fry the sliced vegetables and chopped bacon for 10 min. Boil the stock or tomato juice and add to the vegetables with the nutmeg, lemon juice and herbs and cook for $\frac{3}{4}$–1 hr. Sieve and thicken the soup with $\frac{1}{2}$ oz cornflour or minute tapioca to each 1 pt soup, blended with a little cold milk, stock or water. Stir into the soup, cook till clear, season, add sugar to taste and colouring if needed. Serve garnished like French Onion Soup for a hearty dish.

4–6 helpings

VEGETABLE PURÉES AND CREAM SOUPS

1 lb vegetables	$\frac{1}{4}$ pt milk (*or* $\frac{1}{8}$ pt
Vegetables to	milk and $\frac{1}{8}$ pt
flavour	cream for light-
$\frac{1}{2}$–1 oz butter,	coloured soups)
margarine *or*	$\frac{1}{2}$ oz starchy
other suitable fat	thickening, e.g.
1 pt stock; white	flour, cornflour,
for white and pale	ground rice,
green vegetables;	tapioca *or* potato
brown for dark-	to each pint of
coloured	sieved soup
vegetables; *or*	Salt and pepper
vegetable water	Other flavouring
Flavouring herbs	or colouring if
(optional)	required

Slice or chop the main and flavouring vegetables. Melt the fat in a deep pan and cook the vegetables in it over a gentle heat for 10 min. Keep the lid on the pan and shake it vigorously from time to time. Boil the stock, add it to the vegetables with the herbs and other flavouring (if used) and simmer the whole until the vegetables are quite soft. This cooking time should be as short as possible but will vary with the kind and age of the vegetables used. Remove the herbs, rub or press the vegetables through a sieve (wire for soft, pulpy or very firm vegetables; nylon if a very smooth purée is needed). Mix the liquid with the purée and measure the soup. Weigh or measure the thickening in the proportion given above.

Vegetable purées   Minestrone

Blend the starch powder with the cold milk, stock or water and stir it into the soup. Cook the soup until the starch is thickened and no longer tastes raw. Season carefully to taste.

For a Cream Soup. After the starch thickening has been cooked, remove the pan from the heat. Mix the egg yolk and cream together, stir them into the soup, which should be well below boiling point. Stir over gentle heat till the egg yolk thickens, but *do not boil*. Serve the soup at once; cream and eggs cannot be kept hot.

Cream when used alone may be stirred into the soup just at boiling point, as it is removed from the heat. It must not itself be allowed to boil.

Serve separately: fried croûtons, pulled bread or Melba toast.

HORS D'ŒUVRES

Simple vegetables, fruits (such as apples) and pickles make a colourful selection of hors d'œuvres. They may be uncooked, blanched, or cooked and served cold, and are usually presented in separate small dishes on a tray.

Raw and blanched vegetables should be cut up finely. Carrots should be grated, cabbage finely chopped and cauliflower broken into small sprigs. Other vegetables and fruits often served as part of an hors d'œuvre selection are:

Sliced tomatoes

Sliced cucumber

Diced cooked beetroot

Finely sliced raw onion rings

Cooked green peas with tinned sweetcorn

Shredded green peppers

Diced apple with walnut fragments tossed in lemon juice

Diced new potatoes, 'dressed' while still warm, and cooled

Celery curls

Gherkin fans

Radish roses

Tomato lilies

Small slices or cubes of continental sausage, pâtés or meat may be included. So may sardines and similar fish, and hard-boiled eggs cut in segments. Meat and fish are often sprinkled with chopped parsley to add colour.

Most fruit and vegetable salads are tossed in French Dressing just before serving, to give flavour and to make them more digestible.

Cooked vegetables used as hors d'œuvres should be cooled completely before dressing and serving. They should, like all vegetables, be cooked in as little water as possible and only for just long enough to make them tender. In this way, they retain as much food value as possible, and are crisper and more attractive when mixed with apples and other fruits or meat.

13

HORS D'ŒUVRE VEGETABLES AS TRIMMINGS

Celery Curls Cut celery in 2-in lengths. Shred lengthwise over a coarse grater. Put shreds into iced water and leave for $\frac{1}{2}$ hr.

Gherkin Fans Make about 6 cuts from the top almost to the base of each gherkin. Spread into fan shapes.

Radish Roses Cut off the roots of the radishes. Make 4–6 cuts in each, almost to the base. Put into iced water; they will open like roses.

Tomato Slices and Lilies Slice unskinned tomatoes with a sharp knife. To make lilies, use a stainless steel knife to make zigzag cuts all round the tomato, into the centre. Pull the two halves apart.

Tomatoes, to Skin Drop the tomatoes into hot water for a moment. The skins should then peel off easily.

EGGS À LA DIJON

4 hard-boiled eggs	Tomato garnish

Filling

4 oz cooked ham	Seasoning
2 oz cooked mushrooms	

Cut the eggs in halves, remove the yolks and cut small thin slices off the bottom to make them stand properly. Make a purée of the minced or chopped ham, and mix with the egg yolks and chopped mushrooms and season. Fill the egg whites with the mixture. Garnish with tiny pieces of tomato and serve.

8 savouries

SPICED GRAPEFRUIT

2 large grapefruit	Cherries, glacé or
1 oz butter	Maraschino to
1–2 oz brown sugar	decorate
$\frac{1}{2}$–1 teasp mixed spice	

Halve the grapefruit and loosen the pulp from the skins, discarding pips and pith. Spread with the softened butter and sprinkle sugar and spice over the top. Cook for about 4 min under a hot grill or for 10 min in a fairly hot oven (200 °C, 400 °F, Gas 6). Decorate with cherries and serve at once.

4 helpings

ASPARAGUS WHOLE OR AU NATUREL

1 bundle of asparagus	2 oz butter
Salt	Lemon juice

Trim the hard white ends of the asparagus to suitable lengths for serving. Scrape the stalks with a sharp knife, working downwards from the head. Wash them well in cold water. Tie them into small bundles with the heads in one direction. Re-trim the stalks evenly. Keep them in cold water until ready to cook. Cook very gently, with the heads above the source of heat, in just enough salted boiling water to cover. When tender (in about 15–20 min) drain and serve in a folded table napkin. Serve with melted butter, seasoned and lightly flavoured with lemon.

To ensure that the tender points of the asparagus are not overcooked by the time the stems are ready, the asparagus can be cooked 'standing'. This can be achieved by using a bottling jar half-filled with boiling water, stood in a deep saucepan of boiling water. The asparagus is placed stems down in the jar and the points cook more slowly in steam only.

Allow 30 min for this method of cooking
Allow 6 or 8 medium-sized heads per person

AVOCADO PEARS AND PRAWNS

2 large Avocado pears	2 teacups (about ½ pt) shelled
2 tablesp olive oil	prawns, fresh,
2 tablesp vinegar	frozen or canned
Good pinch of salt	Crisp lettuce
Good pinch of pepper	leaves
A little made mustard	Lemon
	Pinch of sugar (optional)
	¼ crushed clove of garlic (optional)

Halve the pears. Blend the oil, vinegar and seasonings together. Toss the prawns in this, and then spoon into the pear halves. Put on crisp lettuce leaves and garnish with wedges of lemon. A pinch of sugar can be added to the dressing if wished, also a little garlic.

4 helpings

OYSTERS AU NATUREL

To eat oysters 'au naturel' all that is needed, after the shells are opened, is to place the oysters on the upper shell with a little of the liquor; they are then arranged on a dish, garnished with sprigs of fresh parsley, and, if possible, surrounded with ice. Thin slices of buttered brown bread, quarters of lemon and Tabasco sauce can be handed round at the same time; also cayenne pepper and vinegar.

It is advisable to ask the fishmonger to open the shells for you.

Oysters make delicious hot first-course dishes. They can be baked like baked eggs—coquette style, fried in batter or wrapped in strips of bacon, or mixed with a sauce and used as a filling for small vols-au-vent or patty cases. Cheap cooking oysters are not easy to find today, but canned ones can be used instead. (Use canned smoked oysters raw as an hors d'œuvre item. Do not cook them.)

PRAWN OR SHRIMP COCKTAIL

Heart of a small lettuce	1 teasp tarragon vinegar
½ pt shelled prawns *or* shrimps	Good pinch of salt
	Good pinch of cayenne pepper
½ gill mayonnaise	4 prawns in their shells
1 tablesp tomato purée *or*	Brown bread and butter
tomato ketchup	
1 teasp chilli vinegar if available	

Wash and dry the lettuce very well—pick out the tiny leaves and break into very small pieces. Arrange in cocktail glasses. Put the prawns or shrimps on top. Mix the mayonnaise with the tomato ketchup or purée. To obtain the latter, rub one large tomato through a fine sieve. Add the vinegars and seasoning. Put over the shellfish and garnish each glass with an unshelled prawn. Serve with brown bread and butter.

4 helpings

SMOKED FISH

Smoked salmon, trout, buckling, kipper fillets and other smoked fish can be bought at many delicatessen. They make excellent hors d'œuvres.

Have smoked salmon cut thinly from the centre of the salmon. Serve spread on a plate with thin brown bread and butter and lemon wedges. Smoked trout, buckling, etc, are usually served whole but with the heads removed. Sometimes the skin is removed from the top side of the fish too. They are served with salad, bread and butter or toast and lemon wedges.

Kipper fillets, frozen or fresh, are served raw, arranged attractively on a plate, with fresh cream and a garnish of watercress.

SIMPLE HORS D'ŒUVRE SELECTION
Cauliflower sprigs with paprika; smoked
salmon, rolled, with soft cheese; salami
horns; cucumber and cottage cheese rounds;
apple wedges and grated carrot salad

EGGS IN ASPIC

3 hard-boiled eggs	Chervil
1 pt aspic jelly	Cress

Coat the bottoms of 6 dariole moulds with
jelly, decorate them with chervil; when set,
put in slices of egg and aspic jelly alternately,
taking care that each layer of jelly is firmly
set before adding the egg. When the whole
is firmly set, unmould and decorate with
chopped aspic and cress.

LIVER PÂTÉ

1 lb calf's *or* pig's liver *or* the livers from poultry	Pinch of mixed herbs
4 oz very lean ham *or* bacon	A few gherkins (optional)
1 small onion	1–2 hard-boiled eggs (optional)
3 oz butter	A little cream (optional)
Seasoning	Extra butter

Oysters 'au naturel'

above: Asparagus 'au naturel'

below: Eggs in aspic

Cut the liver, ham and onion into small pieces. Heat the butter in a pan and cook the liver, ham and onion for about 6 min— no longer. Put through a very fine mincer twice to give a very smooth mixture. Add the seasoning, herbs and chopped gherkins or chopped hard-boiled eggs too if wished. For a very soft pâté also add a little cream. Put into a dish and cook for about $\frac{1}{2}$ hr in a moderate oven (180 °C, 350 °F, Gas 4),

covering with buttered paper and standing in a dish of cold water to prevent the mixture becoming dry. When the pâté is cooked, cover with a layer of melted butter.

Serve cut in slices on a bed of crisp lettuce and accompanied with hot toast and butter.

4–6 helpings

Breakfast, Brunch and Supper Dishes

POACHED EGGS

To poach well, eggs must be fresh. They should be broken into a cup or saucer and then slipped into boiling salted water to which 1 tablesp vinegar has been added. The water will cease to boil when the eggs are added: do not let it boil again. An average egg will take about 3 min to poach: it is ready when the white has enveloped the yolk and may be touched without breaking. Remove with a perforated spoon.

FRIED EGGS

Method 1 Is for eggs fried on one side only. Melt a little bacon fat or butter in a frying-pan, break the eggs and slip them carefully into the pan. Cook over a gentle heat, basting the eggs with some of the hot fat, until the white is no longer transparent and the yolk is set. Season with pepper and salt.

Method 2 Only one egg can be cooked at a time, but each takes less than one min. Put a teacupful of oil into a small pan so that the egg will actually swim in the oil. Heat until the oil begins to smoke lightly, then maintain this temperature. Break the egg into a cup or saucer and season the yolk with salt and pepper. Slip it quickly into the oil, putting the edge of the cup to the surface of the oil. Dip a smooth wooden spoon into the hot oil, then pull the white over the yolk so as to cover, it completely. Then turn the egg over in the oil and leave for a second only. It will then be done. Remove with a perforated spoon.

FRYING AND GRILLING BACON

Method 1 Cut the rind off the rashers of bacon. Heat the frying-pan for a few minutes. Place the bacon in the hot pan, reduce the heat and cook for a few minutes. Turn the rashers over and continue cooking until the fat is transparent or crisp, as preferred.

Method 2 Cut the rind off the bacon rashers. Place the rashers on the grill rack below the hot grill. After a few minutes' grilling, turn and finish cooking.

SCRAMBLED EGGS

The secret of serving good scrambled eggs lies in slow cooking over a very low. heat (a double saucepan is useful for this), continuous stirring, and immediate serving as the eggs go on cooking in their own heat. It is helpful to add a little butter, or cream, when the scrambling is almost finished: this stops the cooking and improves the flavour, as well as making the texture creamier.

4 eggs	$\frac{1}{2}$ tablesp butter
Salt and pepper	*or* cream
1 tablesp butter	

Break the eggs into a bowl, add seasonings and beat eggs lightly. Meanwhile melt the 1 tablesp butter in the bottom of a pan and roll it around. Before it begins to sizzle pour the eggs into the pan. Reduce the heat to very low, and stir the mixture evenly and constantly with a wooden spoon. When almost ready add about $\frac{1}{2}$ tablesp butter or cream. Remove from the heat as soon as the eggs are set to a soft creamy consistency. Serve immediately.

2 helpings

BAKED EGGS
Heat one cocotte (a special little dish manufactured for this purpose) for each person. Add a little butter or cream, break an egg into each, season to taste, and place the cocottes in a pan of boiling water to come half-way up their sides. Cover the pan and place in a moderate oven (180 °C, 350 °F, Gas 4). Cooking time when the eggs are in thin china dishes will be 6–7 min; allow 8–9 min with thicker dishes.

OMELETS, OMELETTES
There are two types of omelet: the French (sp. omelette), flat and served folded into three, and the English which is fluffy and more like a soufflé.

The essentials in making either type are a thick, clean and dry omelet pan of the right size, i.e. 6–7 in diameter for a 2- or 3-egg omelet; butter; eggs; and seasoning.

For savoury omelets, use one of the two basic types, and fill or stuff the omelet before folding.

FRENCH OMELETTE

2–3 eggs	$\frac{1}{2}$ oz butter
Salt and pepper	

Break the eggs into a basin. Add salt and pepper to taste. Beat the eggs with a fork until they are lightly mixed. Heat the butter in the pan and slowly let it get hot, but not so hot that the butter browns. Without drawing the pan off the heat, pour in the egg mixture. It will cover the pan and start cooking at once.

Shake the pan and stir the eggs with a fork away from the side to the middle. Shake again. In about 1 min the omelette will be soft but no longer runny. Let it stand for 4 or 5 seconds for the bottom to brown slightly. Then remove from the heat. Using a palette knife, fold the omelette from two sides over the middle. Then slip on to a hot dish, or turn it upside down on to the dish.

This omelette can be eaten plain, or it can be filled. There are two methods of filling; flavouring such as herbs or cheese can be added to the eggs after they are beaten, or they can be added to the omelette just before it is folded.

ENGLISH OMELET
Separate the eggs. Add half an egg-shell of water for each egg, to the yolks: beat them with a wooden spoon until creamy. Whisk the whites until they stay in the basin when turned upside down. Gently fold the whites into the yolks. Have the butter ready in the pan as for the French omelette. Pour in the egg mixture, and cook until it is golden brown on the underside. Then put the pan under the grill and lightly brown the top. Fillings are usually spread over the cooked omelet. Now run a palette knife round the edge of the pan. Fold the omelet over and slip on to a hot dish.

SUGGESTED FILLINGS (quantities given are for 2-egg omelettes)
Cheese Grate 2 oz hard cheese finely. Add most of it to the mixed eggs, saving a little to top the finished omelette.

Fines Herbes Finely chop 1 tablesp parsley and a few chives, and add this to the mixed eggs before cooking.

Onion Sauté a large onion in a little butter but do not get it too greasy. When cool, add to the egg mixture, saving a few hot morsels for garnishing the omelette.

Kidney Peel, core and cut 2 lambs' kidneys into smallish pieces, and sauté them in a little butter with a small chopped onion or shallot. Pile this mixture along the centre of the omelette after cooking but before folding.

Mushroom Wash and chop 2 oz mushrooms, sauté them in a little butter until tender. Put them along the centre of the cooked omelette.

Shellfish Shrimps, prawns, crayfish, lobster or crab, fresh or canned, can be used. Chop if necessary and warm slowly through in a little white sauce (or butter) so they are hot when the omelette is cooked. Then pile the mixture along the centre.

Spanish Make a mixture of chopped ham, tomato, sweet pepper, a few raisins, 1 or 2 mushrooms, and sauté in a little butter or olive oil. Add this to the egg before cooking; serve this omelette flat.

For recipes for sweet omelettes, use one of the basic recipes, and fill with fruit purée (*see* Index), jam, or a liqueur-flavoured sweet butter.

CHEESE FONDUE

10–14 oz Emmentaler cheese	1 heaped teasp cornflour *or* potato flour
10–14 oz Gruyère cheese	1 liqueur glass kirsch
1 clove garlic	
4 glasses white wine	Pepper, nutmeg *or* paprika to taste
2–4 teasp lemon juice	

Rub round the inside of an earthenware casserole with garlic and warm up the wine together with the lemon juice. Add the cheese gradually, stirring all the time. Boil up on a good heat, then add the kirsch mixed to a smooth paste with the cornflour. Continue to cook for a short time, stirring the fondue all the time in the form of the figure '8', with a whisk. Stand the fondue on a spirit-stove which can be regulated, so that it continues to boil very slowly. Each person serves himself from the casserole. The creamy cheese mixture is eaten by spearing a cube of bread on a fork, stirring it in the mixture several

Cheese fondue

times, and then transferring the cube to the mouth.

4 helpings

WELSH RAREBIT

1 oz butter *or* margarine	A few drops of Worcester sauce
1 level tablesp flour	4–6 oz grated Cheddar cheese
5 tablesp milk: *or* 3 tablesp milk and 2 tablesp ale *or* beer	Salt and pepper
1 teasp mixed mustard	4 slices of buttered toast

Heat the fat in a pan and stir in the flour.

Scrambled eggs with various additions

Cook for several minutes, stirring well. Add the milk and stir well over the heat until a smooth thick mixture, then add the ale, mustard, Worcester sauce, cheese and a good pinch of salt and pepper. Do not overcook the mixture otherwise the cheese will become 'oily'. Spread on the slices of buttered toast and put under a hot grill until golden brown. Serve at once.

4 helpings or 8 small savouries

SAVOURY BATTER

4 oz flour	**4 tablesp finely**
1 egg	**chopped beef** *or*
$\frac{1}{2}$ pt milk	**mutton**
Salt and pepper	**1 teasp finely**
$\frac{1}{2}$ teasp mixed herbs	**chopped parsley**

Mix the flour, egg, milk, salt and pepper into a smooth batter, let it stand for $\frac{1}{2}$ hr. Then add the meat, parsley and herbs. Melt a little dripping in a Yorkshire pudding tin. Pour in the batter, and bake in a fairly hot oven (190 °C, 375 °F, Gas 5) until set.

2–3 helpings

SAVOURY PANCAKES

1 small onion	**2 tablesp milk**
2 oz cheese	**Salt and pepper**
$\frac{1}{2}$ oz butter *or*	**Batter as for**
margarine	**Savoury Batter**

Grate the onion and cheese. Put into a saucepan, add the butter or margarine and stir in the milk. Season to taste. Heat gently until thoroughly hot.

21

Make the pancakes with the batter, spread with the hot filling and roll up. Serve immediately.

If you prefer, use the same fillings for savoury pancakes as for omelets; see above.

4 helpings

SAUSAGES (COCKTAIL, FRANKFURTER AND LARGE)

Cocktail sausages are best baked. Separate the sausages, prick them with a fork and lay in a baking tin. Bake without extra fat at 180 °C, 350 °F, Gas 4 for about 10 min until brown on top. Turn, and bake a further 7–10 min to brown the underneath.

Frankfurters are treated like large sausages (*see* below). Alternatively, they can be pricked and simmered in white wine with a pinch of thyme until tender (about 10 min).

Large sausages Prick large sausages first with a fork, throw into boiling water and simmer for 15 min. Put into a frying-pan containing a little hot fat, and fry gently, turning to brown on all sides. To fry large sausages, heat slowly to prevent the sausages bursting.

HAMBURGERS

1 lb minced beef	Salt and pepper
$\frac{1}{2}$ cup dry breadcrumbs	1 small onion, minced
$\frac{1}{2}$ cup milk	

Mix together all the ingredients. Form mixture into 6 patties, brown quickly on both sides in hot fat, reduce heat and cook more slowly until done, turning occasionally. Serve in split toasted rolls.

HOT SAVOURY TOASTS

1$\frac{1}{2}$ lb chipolata sausages	2 ripe dessert apples, cored and sliced
5 rashers bacon	
2 tomatoes, sliced	6 slices bread
Sprigs of parsley	1 oz melted butter

Line a grill pan with foil. Cook the sausage and bacon rashers (rolled up) slowly for 10 min under the grill. Add the tomatoes and apple rings. Cut rings from the slices of bread with a plain cutter, and toast them. Brush the tomato and apple slices with melted butter and return to the grill until the apple rings are soft and the whole dish is cooked. Arrange two sausages on each round of toast, top with an apple ring and a slice of tomato. Serve garnished with the bacon rolls and with sprigs of parsley.

3 helpings

MACARONI AU GRATIN WITH BACON ROLLS

4 oz macaroni	Browned bread-crumbs *or* 1 oz finely grated Cheddar cheese
1 pt white sauce	
4 oz grated cheese	
Bacon rashers	
Salt and pepper	Butter

Break the macaroni into pieces about 1$\frac{1}{2}$ in long, put them into rapidly boiling salted water and boil for about 20 min, or until the macaroni is tender. (If not required for immediate use, cover the macaroni with cold water to prevent the pieces sticking together.) Cover the bottom of a well-buttered baking dish with white sauce, sprinkle liberally with cheese, seasoning to taste, and add a layer of macaroni. Repeat the layers, cover the last layer of macaroni thickly with sauce, sprinkle the surface lightly with breadcrumbs or extra grated cheese and add a few small pieces of butter. Bake in a hot oven (220 °C, 425 °F, Gas 7) for about 20 min.

Cut the rind off the rashers, roll each one up and place in a baking tin with the cut ends underneath. Bake under the macaroni dish for 10–15 min until the bacon rolls are crisp. Use as a garnish, or serve separately.

6–7 helpings

Sandwiches and Savoury Pastries

SANDWICHES

The term 'sandwich' has a much wider meaning today than when it was first introduced by the Earl of Sandwich, and applied only to slices of meat placed between bread and butter. We have now 'Open' or Continental sandwiches and attractively shaped Party sandwiches. Their fillings are now immensely varied, savoury or sweet, minced or shredded and mixed with various butters, sauces and seasonings.

Making sandwiches requires little skill, just plenty of imagination and an eye for colour.

For sandwiches the bread should be fresh but not too new; French rolls, Vienna rolls, wholemeal or milk bread make an interesting change from ordinary loaves. Creamed butter is more easily spread than ordinary butter. When ordinary butter is used it should first be beaten to a cream (add 1 teasp hot water to $\frac{1}{2}$ lb butter) to make spreading easier. Savoury butters give piquancy and variety to other fillings, and can be used alone for rolled sandwiches.

Sandwiches simplify entertaining, for they can be prepared well in advance and can be served buffet-style, leaving the hostess free to mix with her guests. If prepared some time before required, sandwiches keep fresh and moist if wrapped in greaseproof paper and then in a damp cloth, or if put into a polythene bag, or wrapped in waxed paper or aluminium foil, and kept in the fridge or a cool place. Sandwiches with different fillings should be wrapped separately to prevent the flavours mixing.

SANDWICH FILLINGS
Savoury fillings

1 Anchovies mixed with hard-boiled egg yolk, cheese and butter, with a sprinkling of cayenne. Spread the bread with curry butter.

2 Canned tuna fish mixed with salad cream, and chopped parsley, with a dash of cayenne.

3 Canned salmon, mashed with lemon juice and chopped chives, spread on a bed of cucumber slices.

4 Minced cooked smoked haddock, seasoned and mixed to a smooth paste with butter and anchovy paste.

5 Very thin slices of cooked chicken and ham, seasoned and placed between bread spread with curry butter.

6 Very finely shredded celery, moistened slightly with canned or double cream, seasoned to taste.

7 Finely grated cheese, mixed to a smooth paste with a little seasoning, anchovy essence or paste, and butter.

8 A layer of finely chopped gherkin, olives and capers, mixed with mayonnaise sauce, covered with a layer of full-fat soft cheese.

9 Mashed sardines, a little lemon juice and seasoning, mixed to a smooth paste with butter.

10 Sardines mashed with an equal amount of grated cheese until smooth; seasoned to taste, with a little lemon juice or vinegar added and sufficient cream or milk to moisten.

11 Minced cooked chicken and ham or tongue, combined with full-fat soft cheese and egg yolk, seasoned and moistened with oil.

12 Finely shredded lettuce and watercress, seasoned with salt and mixed with mayonnaise.

top left: Macaroni au gratin with bacon rolls   top right: Sausage rolls

below: Cold table with open sandwiches

13 Thin slices of Gruyère cheese on slices of bread and butter, spread with French mustard, seasoned with pepper.

14 Slices of hard-boiled egg, seasoned, covered with watercress or mustard and cress, sprinkled with equal quantities of oil and vinegar.

15 Canned foie gras.

16 Minced cooked chicken and ham or tongue, moistened with a little liquid butter and mayonnaise.

17 Lightly spread caviare, sprinkled with lemon juice and a little cayenne. The bread may be spread with shrimp butter.

25

Sweet fillings

1 Bananas mashed with lemon juice and ground almonds and sprinkled with sugar.

2 A layer of full-fat soft cheese or cottage cheese, covered with a layer of fresh strawberries or raspberries sprinkled with castor sugar.

3 Softened creamed cheese, mixed with canned crushed pineapple and finely chopped preserved ginger.

4 Chocolate spread, mixed with chopped walnuts and cottage cheese.

5 Chopped pears, dates and walnuts, mixed with golden syrup.

6 Thick slices of banana sprinkled with coarsely grated chocolate.

OPEN SANDWICHES

Use $\frac{1}{4}$-in thick slices of white or brown bread. Spread with softened butter, and with any of the party sandwich fillings below. Garnish with stuffed olives, slices of hard-boiled egg, small pieces of tomato, watercress, piped creamed cheese, etc.

The appeal of these sandwiches lies in the artistic way in which the garnish is arranged. They must look colourful, fresh and tempting. Remember that garnishes stay fresher if arranged vertically, and if kept under damp paper or cloth until serving time.

Savoury Scandinavian garnishes

1 Samsöe cheese with radish.

2 Tongue with Russian salad, cucumber and a twist of tomato.

3 Egg and crisply fried bacon, with cucumber and a twist of tomato.

4 Liver pâté with mushrooms sautéed in butter, shreds of crisply fried bacon, tomato, lettuce and gherkin.

5 Pork luncheon meat with horseradish cream, and an orange butterfly.

6 Danish blue cheese with black grapes.

7 Salami (without garlic) with raw onion rings and chopped parsley.

8 Pork luncheon meat with young carrots, peas in mayonnaise and cucumber.

9 Danish blue cheese with chopped apple coated with French dressing, topped with a parsley sprig.

TWO-DECKER SANDWICHES

Either brown or white bread may be used for club or double-decker sandwiches. Cut the slices thinly—three slices for each sandwich. Butter the slices thickly—the middle slice should be buttered on both sides—spread with 2 fillings and sandwich together. Press together firmly so that the layers stick to each other. These sandwiches may be served plain or toasted, hot or cold, and knives and forks should be provided.

Fillings

1 *1st layer* Slices of cold roast beef, seasoned and spread with horseradish sauce.

2nd layer Watercress with thin slices of drained, pickled beetroot.

2 *1st layer* A slice of Cheddar cheese spread with mango chutney.

2nd layer A mixture of grated raw apple and mayonnaise.

3 *1st layer* Cooked skinless pork sausage split lengthwise.

2nd layer Grilled mushrooms.

TOASTED SANDWICHES

Toasted sandwiches make excellent dishes for TV or late-night suppers, and are economical to produce since leftovers can often be used.

To make them, you can toast the bread on both sides, butter one side of each slice and fill with a hot or cold, separately prepared filling.

Alternatively, toast the bread slices by grilling, on one side only. Spread a suitable filling, such as grated cheese mixed with apple slices and peanut butter, all over the untoasted side. Make sure the filling covers the bread. Grill the filling until crisp or bubbling. Top with a piece of bread toasted on both sides and decorate to choice; for instance, with fried or raw onion rings, tomato slices and watercress. (*See also* Hot Vol-au-Vent fillings below.)

PASTRY CASES

Vol-au-vent or patty cases filled with savoury mixtures are excellent for first courses and also for TV suppers and for buffet parties. They can be served hot or cold. If a mixture is being put into cold pastry cases, make sure it is quite cold. If, on the other hand, it is being put into hot pastry cases, heat the filling and the pastry separately, and put together at the last minute, so that the filling does not make the pastry soft.

Vol-au-vent cases can be bought uncooked, frozen, or ready to use. They can also, of course, be made at home, using frozen or home-made puff pastry.

HOT VOL-AU-VENT OR TOASTED SANDWICH FILLINGS

Hot vols-au-vent and toasted sandwiches (*see* above) cannot have fillings which melt easily and run out of the casing. Here are types of fillings from which you can develop others:

Chicken filling

1 × 3 oz pkt full-fat soft cheese	1 small onion, peeled and sliced
1 chicken joint, cooked	

Divide the cheese into 6 portions (for two sandwiches or 6 vols-au-vent). Cut the chicken into bite-sized pieces. Fry the onion rings gently until tender.

On two slices of bread or in 6 vols-au-vent, lay (a) onion rings (b) a little cheese. Lay on these two more slices of bread if making sandwiches. Add the chicken and remaining cheese. Top sandwiches with a third slice of bread each, vols-au-vent with 'hats'. Toast sandwiches on both sides, and heat vols-au-vent in a gentle oven.

Bacon and mushroom filling

6 rashers streaky bacon	$\frac{1}{4}$ lb mushrooms, sautéed in butter
1 × 3 oz pkt full-fat soft cheese	Salt and pepper

Chop the bacon and fry until crisp. Chop the mushrooms and add them. Season, and cool.

Mix half the cheese with the bacon bits, and half with the mushrooms. Spread bacon and cheese between two slices of bread or in the lower halves of 6 vols-au-vent. Top each second slice of bread or fill the upper half of each vol-au-vent with the mushroom–cheese mixture. Top with two more slices of bread or vol-au-vent 'hats'. Toast or heat as in previous recipe.

SAUSAGE ROLLS

Puff pastry, frozen *or* **using 4 oz of flour etc if home-made**	$\frac{1}{2}$ **lb sausages** **Egg yolk to glaze**

Roll out the pastry and cut into 8 even-sized squares. Skin the sausages. Divide the sausage meat into 8 portions and make each piece into a roll the same length as the pastry. Place the sausage meat on the pastry, wet the edge and fold over leaving the ends open. Knock up the edges with the back of a knife. Make three incisions on top. Brush over with beaten egg and place on a baking-sheet. Bake in a hot oven (220 °C, 425 °F, Gas 7) until the pastry is well risen and brown. Reduce the heat and continue baking till the pastry is cooked.

Small sausage rolls can be quickly made by rolling the pastry into an oblong. Form the sausage meat into long rolls the length of the pastry, then divide the pastry into strips wide enough to encircle the meat. Damp one edge of each strip, fold over and press together firmly. Cut into rolls of the desired length, and finish as above.

Home-made sausage 'spiral' rolls are a decorative alternative. Use whole small sausages with skins. Roll out the pastry into a long strip about $\frac{1}{2}$ in wide. Wrap pastry strip diagonally round and round each sausage leaving a small gap between strip edges. Bake as above.

Fish Dishes

BAKED HADDOCK AND ORANGE

1 orange	2 level teasp
1½ lb fillet of	cornflour
haddock	½ level teasp
Salt	sugar
Juice of 1 lemon	

Grate the rind from the orange, remove the pith and cut pulp across into slices. Cut the fish into convenient portions for serving. Arrange in a greased dish. Sprinkle with a little salt, add the lemon juice and arrange the slices of orange over the top. Cover with greased paper and cook in a fairly hot oven (200 °C, 400 °F, Gas 6) for 15–20 min. Strain off the liquor and make up to ¼ pt with water. Blend the cornflour with this, add the grated orange rind and sugar, and bring to the boil, stirring constantly. Boil gently for 3 min, correct the seasoning and serve with the fish.

4 helpings

BAKED FROZEN HADDOCK FILLETS WITH CUCUMBER SAUCE

1 × 13-oz carton	½ pt milk
frozen haddock	Salt and pepper
fillets	Cucumber sauce

Partially thaw and separate the fillets into suitable portions for serving. Place in a baking tin, cover with the milk, season and bake for 20 min in a fairly hot oven (190 °C, 375 °F, Gas 5). When cooked, place the fillets on a serving-dish and keep warm while making the Cucumber Sauce. Pour the sauce over the fish before serving.

SOLE À LA PORTUGAISE

1 medium-sized	1 onion
sole	2–3 tomatoes
1 oz butter	1 dessertsp
1 shallot	grated Parmesan
1 teasp finely	cheese
chopped parsley	1 dessertsp
½ teasp anchovy	browned bread-
essence	crumbs
Salt and pepper	Extra butter

Skin the sole and make an incision down the centre as for filleting; raise the flesh from the bone on each side as far as possible. Mix the butter, finely chopped shallot, parsley and anchovy essence well together, and stuff the mixture inside the sole. Place the fish in a buttered fireproof dish, season. Arrange slices of onion and tomato alternately and overlapping each other, on top of the fish;

or if less onion is preferred, surround each slice of tomato with a single ring of onion. Mix together the cheese and breadcrumbs and sprinkle over the fish. Place small pieces of butter on top, cover with lid or greased paper and bake for about 20 min in a moderate oven (180 °C, 350 °F, Gas 4).

Fillets of sole can be laid on a bed of the stuffing and cooked in the same way. Omit the onion and tomato rings if desired.

2 helpings

SOLE OR PLAICE AUX FINES HERBES

Eight 2-oz fillets of sole or plaice 4 tablesp fish stock or court bouillon ½ pt white wine sauce	1 tablesp finely chopped fresh herbs Salt and pepper

Wipe the fillets with a clean, damp cloth, season with salt and pepper and fold them in three. Place in a greased fireproof dish, add the stock or court bouillon, and cook in a fairly hot oven (190 °C, 375 °F, Gas 5) for 15–20 min. Drain the fillets well and place on a dish, coat with white wine sauce and sprinkle with the finely chopped fresh herbs. Whole skinned whiting can also be used for this dish.

4 helpings

POACHED COD À LA PROVENÇALE

2 lb middle cut cod (approx) Salt and pepper ½ pt Velouté or other rich white sauce 1 gill white stock 2 small shallots A small bunch of parsley Bouquet garni	1 egg yolk 2 oz butter 1 teasp anchovy paste 1 teasp chopped parsley 2 teasp capers

Wash and wipe the fish well and place in a saucepan. Season with pepper and salt, and add the sauce, stock, finely chopped shallots,

bunch of parsley and the bouquet garni. Simmer slowly until the fish is done, basting occasionally. Remove the fish to a hot dish, and keep it warm. Reduce the sauce until the desired consistency is obtained. Remove the herbs, add the egg yolk, work in the butter, and pass through a strainer. Return to a smaller saucepan, add the anchovy paste, chopped parsley and capers, stir over heat for a few minutes but do not allow to boil, then pour over the fish.

5–6 helpings   Cooking time 35–40 min

POACHED HALIBUT OR TURBOT STEAKS WITH PRAWN SAUCE

3–4 halibut or turbot steaks Salt	½ pt anchovy, prawn or shrimp sauce

Add salt to hot water in the proportion of 1 oz to 1 qt, and put in the fish. Bring slowly to boiling point and simmer very gently until cooked through, about 12–15 min. Drain well, arrange in a hot dish and pour the sauce over. Garnish with unshelled, cooked prawns or shrimps if desired.

3–4 helpings

BOILED OR POACHED SALMON AND SALMON TROUT

Make a court bouillon in a fish-kettle or large pan, using just enough water to cover the fish. Wash, clean and scale the fish. Remove the gills, intestines and eyes, but leave on the head and tail. Tie loosely in a piece of muslin if using a stewpan. Remove any scum on the court bouillon, then gently put in the fish and boil (or rather poach) until cooked through. The time will depend on the size and thickness of the fish. Allow 10 min per lb for a thick fish, or whole salmon trout, and 7 min for a tail piece of salmon.

Arrange on a flat dish, garnish with sliced cucumber, parsley, lemon and new potatoes. Serve with melted butter or Hollandaise sauce.

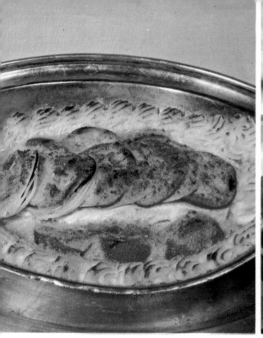

Sole à la Portugaise

Plaice mornay

FILLETS OF SOLE BONNE FEMME

4 fillets of sole	A little butter
4 oz mushrooms	
1 shallot	
1 teasp chopped parsley	
Salt and pepper	
$\frac{1}{4}$ pt white wine	
$\frac{1}{4}$ pt Velouté sauce	

Wipe the fillets with a clean damp cloth. Put them flat in a shallow pan with the sliced mushrooms, sliced shallot, parsley and seasoning. Add the wine, cover and poach for 10–15 min. Drain the fish from the wine, place on a fireproof dish and keep warm. Boil the wine rapidly until it is reduced by half, then stir it into the hot Velouté sauce and thicken with a little butter. When thoroughly blended pour the sauce over the fillets and place under a hot grill until lightly browned. Serve at once in a border of sliced, steamed potatoes.

4 helpings

PLAICE MORNAY

Four 4-oz fillets of plaice, fresh or frozen

Sauce

1 oz butter	2 tablesp grated
1 rounded tablesp flour	Gruyère or Cheddar cheese
Salt and pepper	Mustard
$\frac{1}{2}$ pt milk and fish stock mixed	Grated nutmeg

Fold the fillets in half and steam between 2 plates. Meanwhile make the sauce by melting the fat in a small saucepan, adding the flour, a pinch of salt and pepper, and cooking for 2–3 min without browning. Remove from heat and stir in the liquid gradually, mixing well to prevent lumpiness. Bring to the boil, still stirring, and cook for 5 min. Add most of the cheese and season with mustard and nutmeg. Arrange the cooked fish in a shallow fireproof dish, coat with sauce and sprinkle with the remaining cheese. Place under a hot grill until golden brown. Serve with grilled or baked tomatoes and mashed potatoes.

4 helpings

32

Grilled herrings with mustard sauce

Poached halibut with prawn sauce

STEAMED WHITING

1 whiting
Salt and pepper
Lemon juice
White sauce

Skin the whiting and curl it with its tail in its mouth. (Your fishmonger will do this for you.) Place it in a well-buttered soup plate, sprinkle lightly with salt, pepper and lemon juice, and cover with a generously buttered paper. Have ready a saucepan containing boiling water, place the plate on top of it and cover with another plate or the lid of the saucepan. Cook for 20–25 min, turning the fish once during the process. Serve with its own liquid or with white sauce.

Sole or plaice can be steamed in the same way, but take only 10–12 min. These are suitable dishes for invalids.

1 helping

SMOKED HADDOCK

Smoked haddock is best cooked either in the oven or on the top of the cooker in a dish with a little water to create steam, and so to prevent the surface of the fish becoming hardened. Medium-sized haddocks should be cooked whole, and before serving an incision should be made from head to tail and the backbone removed. The fish should be liberally spread with butter, sprinkled with pepper and served as hot as possible.

KEDGEREE

1 lb cold cooked fish (smoked haddock is generally preferred)	**$\frac{1}{4}$ lb rice**
	2 hard-boiled eggs
	2 oz butter
	Salt and pepper
	Cayenne pepper

Boil and dry the rice. Divide the fish into small flakes. Cut the whites of the eggs into slices and sieve the yolks. Melt the butter in a saucepan, add to it the fish, rice, egg whites, salt, pepper and cayenne and stir until hot.

Turn the mixture on to a hot dish. Press into the shape of a pyramid with a fork, decorate with egg yolk and serve as hot as possible.

5–6 helpings   Cooking time 40–50 min

FISH CAKES

1 lb cooked fish	2 eggs
1 oz butter *or* margarine	Salt and pepper
$\frac{1}{2}$ lb mashed potatoes	Breadcrumbs

Remove skin and bones and chop fish coarsely. Heat the butter in a saucepan, add the fish, potatoes, yolk of 1 egg, salt and pepper. Stir over heat for a few minutes, then turn on to a plate and allow to cool. When cold, shape into round flat cakes, brush over with beaten egg, coat with breadcrumbs and fry in hot fat. The fish may be made into one large cake instead of several small ones, in which case grease a fish mould or flat tin and shape the mixture as much like a fish as possible. Brush over with egg, cover with slightly browned breadcrumbs and bake for about 20 min in a fairly hot oven (190 °C, 375 °F, Gas 5).

3–7 helpings

CAPKIN OR MIXED FISH GRILL

Four 4–5-oz portions sea bream, coley, hake, brill *or* cod	1 level dessertsp chopped pickled capers
2 tablesp salad oil	1 level dessertsp chopped pickled gherkins
1 tablesp vinegar	1 level dessertsp chopped parsley
Salt and pepper to taste	

Prepare the fish and place skin side uppermost in the grill pan. Mix together all the other ingredients except the parsley, and pour over the fish. Grill for about 12–15 min, turning once and basting frequently with the sauce. Serve hot, sprinkled with parsley.

4 helpings

JUGGED AND GRILLED KIPPERS

1–2 kippers per person	Slices of lemon
Butter *or* margarine	Parsley sprigs

To jug Kippers

Simply place the kippers in a tall jug and cover with boiling water. Cover the jug and stand it in a warm place for 5–10 min. Drain, and serve with a knob of butter or margarine on each kipper. This method produces plump, juicy kippers, though some say a little flavour is lost.

To grill Kippers

Remove the heads and lay the kippers flat, skin side up, on the grid. Cook for about 3 min each side, adding a dab of butter or margarine when they are turned over. Top with a slice of lemon decorated with parsley. Serve alone or on a slice of toast.

Alternatively, place a pair of kippers, flesh sides together, and grill under medium heat first on one side then on the other; to serve, separate and top each with a slice of lemon or nut of butter.

GRILLED MACKEREL WITH GOOSEBERRY SAUCE

2 large mackerel	$\frac{1}{2}$ lb gooseberries *or* a small bottle *or* 10-oz can of gooseberries
1 tablesp seasoned flour	
1 oz margarine	
2 *or* 3 tomatoes	$\frac{1}{4}$ level teasp grated nutmeg

Trim, clean and fillet the mackerel. Dip each fillet in seasoned flour. Melt the margarine in the bottom of the grill pan, add the fillets, brush them with the melted fat and grill for 8–10 min, turning once. Cut the tomatoes in half and grill at the same time, for garnish.

Meanwhile prepare the gooseberries. Stew in a very little water, or in their own juice if bottled or canned. Sweeten slightly if necessary, rub through a sieve and return the purée to the pan. Stir in the grated nutmeg and reheat (reduce by rapid boiling if necessary). Serve the fillets on a hot dish, garnished with the tomatoes and serve the sauce separately.

Grilled mackerel may be served with Maître d'Hôtel butter or Maître d'Hôtel sauce if preferred to gooseberry sauce.

4 helpings

GRILLED HERRINGS WITH MUSTARD SAUCE

4 fresh herrings	$\frac{1}{2}$ oz flour
Melted butter *or*	1 teasp dry
cooking oil	mustard
1 onion	$\frac{1}{2}$ pt vinegar
1 oz butter	

Wipe and dry the herrings, remove the heads and score across the back and sides. Avoid cutting the roe. Sprinkle with salt and pepper, brush very lightly with melted butter or oil and grill under a very hot grill for 8–12 min, turning once. Place on a hot dish and garnish with lemon wedges and fresh green parsley. Serve the sauce separately.

Mustard sauce
Chop the onion finely and fry in the butter until lightly browned. Put in the flour and mustard, add the vinegar and $\frac{1}{4}$ pt water. Stir until boiling and simmer gently for 15 min.

3–4 helpings

FILLETS OF PLAICE WITH LEMON DRESSING

4 fillets of plaice	Juice of $\frac{1}{2}$ lemon
(4 oz each approx)	Chopped parsley
Seasoning	
1 oz butter *or*	
margarine	

Season the fish. Melt the fat in the grill pan and place the fish skin side uppermost in the pan. Cook for 1 min, then turn with flesh side up and grill steadily until golden-brown and cooked, about 5–8 min, depending on thickness of fillets. Remove to a hot serving-dish, keep hot. Add the lemon juice to the remaining fat in the pan, reheat and pour over the fish. Sprinkle liberally with chopped parsley.

4 helpings

GRILLED SALMON

2–3 slices of	1 tablesp (about
salmon (middle	1 oz) Maître
cut) about $\frac{3}{4}$ in	d'Hôtel *or*
thick	anchovy butter
2 tablesp olive	Parsley
oil *or* oiled butter	Lemon (optional)
(approx)	
Salt and pepper	

Wipe the fish with a damp cloth, then brush over with oil or oiled butter. Season to taste with salt and pepper and place the slices on a well-greased grill rack. Grill each side for 6–8 min, according to the thickness of the slices. When done, place the fish on a flat dish, and place pat of Maître d'Hôtel or anchovy butter on each slice. Garnish with sprigs of fresh parsley. Serve hot.

4–6 helpings

TROUT MEUNIÈRE

4 large *or*	1 tablesp lemon
8 small trout	juice
A little	1 level tablesp
seasoned flour	chopped parsley
3 oz butter	Lemon
	'butterflies'

Dredge the trout lightly, but thoroughly, with seasoned flour. Heat the butter in a frying-pan and when hot fry the trout until golden-brown and cooked through. Arrange the trout on a hot dish. Reheat the fat until it is nut brown in colour and then pour it over the fish. Sprinkle the lemon juice and parsley over the fish, garnish with lemon 'butterflies' and serve at once.

4 helpings

CHEQUERBOARD SALAD

1 lb cod fillet *or*	Salt and pepper
other white fish	Lettuce leaves
2 tablesp water	1 small can (2 oz)
2 tablesp lemon	anchovy fillets
juice	Hard-boiled egg
1 level tablesp	*or* olives
chopped parsley	
1 level tablesp	
chopped chives	

Place the fish in a fireproof dish with the water. Cover and cook in a fairly hot oven (190 °C, 375 °F, Gas 5) for 20 min. Allow to cool. Remove any skin and bones, flake the fish, then moisten it with the lemon juice and stir in the parsley and chives with seasoning to taste. Arrange neatly on a bed of shredded lettuce, flattening and smoothing the top. Place the anchovy fillets diagonally on top in a squared pattern, filling the spaces with rings of hard-boiled egg or slices of stoned olives. Garnish with radish roses and parsley.

4 helpings

'GEFILTE' FISH

$2-2\frac{1}{2}$ **lb fish**
2–3 onions
1–2 sticks of
celery
1 large carrot
Salt and pepper
1 tablesp chopped
parsley
2 eggs
Fresh
breadcrumbs

Remove the skin and bones from the fish and put them in a saucepan with 1 onion, the celery and a piece of carrot; pour $1\frac{1}{2}$ pt water over, season with salt and pepper. Cover and simmer gently for $\frac{1}{2}$ hr, then strain. Put the fish and remaining onion through the mincing-machine or chop finely by hand. Add the parsley and beaten eggs to the chopped fish; season with salt and pepper and add sufficient fresh breadcrumbs to bind. With floured hands roll into balls. Slice the carrot thinly, add to the fish stock and bring to the boil; then put in the fish balls, cover and simmer very gently for 1 hr. Lift the balls out carefully on to a serving-dish and place a slice of carrot on top of each. Spoon over a little of the fish stock and serve cold, when the stock should have set in a jelly.

This dish originated in the East, where salt-water fish is in short supply, and was made from pike and carp. But bream, cod, haddock or a mixture can be used.

5–6 helpings   Cooking time about $1\frac{1}{2}$ hr

above: Grilled salmon cutlets

below: Chequerboard salad

POACHED SALMON AND SALMON TROUT SERVED COLD

Cool the fish a little after cooking. Neatly remove the skin from one side. Serve quite plain, on a bed of decorated aspic jelly, and garnish with unshelled prawns. Use slices of stuffed olive to fill the eye sockets.

Alternatively, glaze the cold fish with aspic jelly made with liquor in which the fish was cooked. Garnish with chopped aspic, tomato segments and sliced cucumber.

36

above: Fried plaice with lemon   below: Salmon mousse

SALMON MOUSSE WITH ASPIC

1 lb cooked
salmon (approx)
or **one 20-oz can**
1 oz gelatine
1 pt fish stock
Salt and pepper
½ cucumber,
sliced
A few slices
tomato

Dissolve the gelatine in the stock and season to taste. Drain the oil from the salmon and remove all skin and bones. Cover the bottom of a mould with the jellied stock, let it set, and then decorate with slices of cucumber. Set the garnish with a little jelly. Allow to set. Add a layer of salmon, cover with jelly and put aside until set. Repeat until the mould is full. Keep in the fridge or in a cool place until wanted, then turn out. Garnish the dish with sliced cucumber and tomato. 1 tablesp sherry or Marsala can be added to the jelly for flavour.

6–8 helpings

37

SHELLFISH DISHES

PREPARING CRAB

After wiping well with a damp cloth, place the crab on its back with the tail facing you, and remove claws and legs by twisting them in the opposite way to which they lie. Place the thumbs under flap at tail and push upwards, pull flap away upwards so that the stomach contents are not drawn over the meat, and lift off. (The fishmonger will do this on request.) Reverse the crab so that the head is facing, then press on the mouth with the thumbs, pushing down and forward; the mouth and stomach will then come away in one piece. Remove the meat from the shell by easing round the inside edge of the shell to loosen the tissues with the handle of a plastic teaspoon, and the meat will then come away easily. Keep the dark and the white meat separate. With the handle of a knife, tap sharply over the false line round the shell cavity, press down and it will come away neatly. Scrub and dry the shell, then rub over with a little oil. Remove the 'deadmen's fingers' (the lungs) and discard, then scoop out the meat from the claw sockets. Scoop out as much as possible but keep it free of bone. Twist off first joint of large claws and scoop out meat. Tap sharply round the broad shell with back of knife and halves fall apart. Cut the cartilage between the pincers, open pincers and meat will come away in one piece.

CURRIED CRAB

1 good-sized crab	1 oz butter *or* other good cooking fat
Mustard	
1 shallot *or* onion	$\frac{1}{2}$ pt curry sauce
$\frac{1}{2}$ apple	4 oz plain boiled rice

Remove the meat from the crab, including the claws, flake it up and sprinkle a little dry mustard over it. Peel and finely chop the shallot or onion; peel, core and chop the apple. Melt the butter in a saucepan and lightly fry the shallot and apple. Fry for a few minutes only, then add the curry sauce and lastly the crab meat. Re-heat and serve on a hot dish in the centre of a border of rice.

3–4 helpings

SCALLOPED CRAB

1 medium-sized crab	Vinegar
Fine breadcrumbs	A little white sauce
Salt and pepper	Butter
Mustard	

Remove the meat from the claws and body of the crab. Add about half its bulk in breadcrumbs, season with salt, pepper and mustard, and stir in a few drops of vinegar. Add white sauce to moisten, then turn into buttered scallop shells and sprinkle the surface lightly with breadcrumbs. Place small pieces of butter on top and bake in a moderate oven (180 °C, 350 °F, Gas 4) until nicely browned—about 15 min.

4–5 helpings

DRESSED CRAB IN SHELL

One $2\frac{1}{2}$–3 lb crab	A little lemon juice (optional)
Salt and pepper	French dressing
Fresh breadcrumbs (optional)	

Pick the crab meat from the shells. Mix the dark crab meat with salt and pepper, fresh breadcrumbs and a little lemon juice if liked. The breadcrumbs are optional but they lessen the richness and give a firmer texture. Press the mixture lightly against the sides of the previously cleaned shell. Flake up the white meat, mix with French dressing and pile in the centre of the shell. Garnish with sieved egg yolk, chopped egg white, chopped parsley, sieved coral if any, and decorate with small claws. Make a necklace with the small claws, place on a dish and rest the crab on this. Surround with salad.

4 helpings

CRAB SALAD

1 large cooked crab *or* 2 small cooked crabs *or* 6 oz crab meat	1 dessertsp chopped parsley Salt and pepper Crisp lettuce
2 celery hearts *or* the heart of 1 endive	leaves 2 hard-boiled eggs 1 tablesp capers
2 tablesp olive oil 2 tablesp tarragon vinegar 1 tablesp chilli *or* caper vinegar	12 stoned olives Anchovy butter

Cut the meat of the crabs into convenient-sized pieces. Shred the celery or endive, add to the crab meat and mix lightly with the oil, vinegar, parsley and seasoning. Serve on a bed of lettuce leaves; garnish with slices of hard-boiled egg, capers and olives stuffed with anchovy butter.

6 helpings

PREPARING AND COOKING CRAWFISH AND CRAYFISH

Crawfish are what the French call *langoustes*. They are treated just like lobsters. Crayfish are fresh-water shellfish, also like lobsters but much smaller. They are greenish-brown above, yellowish beneath, but turn red when boiled. They are in season from June to March. The French call them *écrevisses*. To cook crayfish, wash thoroughly, remove intestinal cord and throw the fish into boiling, salted water. Boil for 10–15 min according to size.

BOILING A LOBSTER

There are two methods of boiling lobsters, each method having points in its favour.

Method 1 Wash the lobster well before boiling, tie the claws securely. Have ready a saucepan of boiling water, salted in the proportion of $\frac{1}{4}$ lb salt to 1 gallon water. Throw the lobster head first into the water (this instantly destroys life), keep it boiling for 20–45 min, according to size, and skim well. Allow 20 min–$\frac{1}{2}$ hr for small lobsters and $\frac{1}{2}$–$\frac{3}{4}$ hr for large lobsters. If boiled too long the meat becomes thready, and if not done enough, the coral is not red. If serving in the shell, rub the shells over with a little salad oil to brighten the colour.

Method 2 Put the lobster into warm water, bring the water gradually to the boil and boil as above. This is believed by many to be a more humane method of killing, as the lobster is lulled to sleep and does not realize it is being killed.

PREPARING A LOBSTER

Wipe the lobster well with a clean damp cloth and twist off claws and legs. Place lobster on a board parallel to the edge with back uppermost and head to the left. Cut along the centre of back, from junction of head with body to tail, using a sharp, stainless knife. Reverse so that tail is to left and cut along head; the stomach, which lies just behind the mouth, is not cut until last. Remove intestinal cord, remove stomach and coral (if any) and keep for garnish. The meat may be left in the shell or removed and used as required. To remove claw meat, knock tips of the claws with the back of a knife and drain away any water. Tap sharply round the broadest part of each claw and the shell should fall apart. Cut the cartilage between pincers, open the pincers and the meat can be removed in one piece. Remove the meat from the smaller joints of claws.

LOBSTER THERMIDOR

2 small boiled lobsters	1 level teasp mixed mustard
1 shallot	Pinch of cayenne
1 wine glass white wine	pepper A little grated
$1\frac{1}{2}$ oz butter	cheese
$\frac{1}{4}$ pt Béchamel sauce	Parsley to garnish

Cut the lobsters in half lengthwise and remove the stomach and the intestinal cord. Remove the meat from the shell and cut into slices, keeping the knife on the slant. Chop the shallot very finely. Put the white wine in a small saucepan and cook the shallot until it is tender and the wine reduced to half. Meanwhile, melt the butter and heat the meat very carefully in this. Add the shallot and wine mixture to the lobster meat with the sauce, mustard and pepper, mix

Lobster thermidor

and return to the shells. Sprinkle with grated cheese and brown under a hot grill. Serve garnished with parsley and accompanied by a simple salad or plain lettuce.

4 helpings

DRESSED LOBSTER

Prepare the boiled lobster as described above. Leave the meat in the shell and arrange each half on a bed of salad. Garnish with the

Dressed lobster

claws. Serve with oil and vinegar handed separately. Piped lobster butter may be used to garnish the shell, if wished. Dressed crab also makes a luxurious main dish for a summer meal. It is prepared and garnished in the same way as lobster.

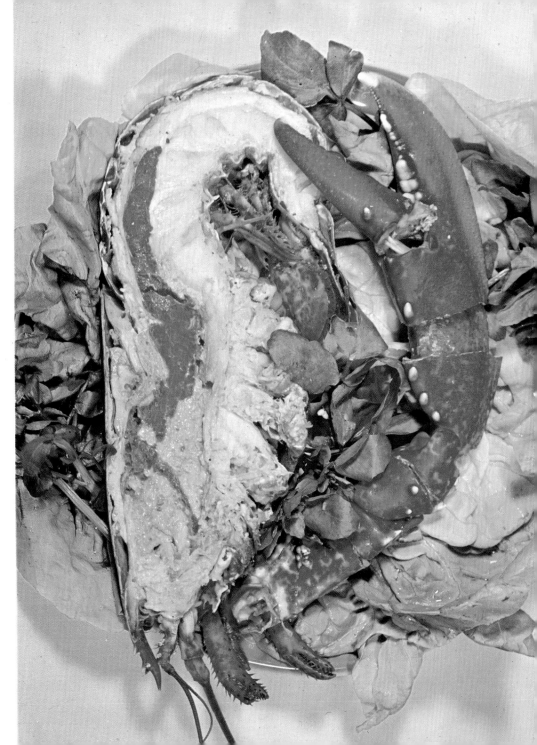

OYSTERS AND THEIR PREPARATION

Oysters have the highest reputation of all shellfish. English oysters are in season locally from September to the end of April, and the best kind to get, to eat *au naturel* are the large flavoursome, Whitstable or Colchester 'natives'. Smaller foreign oysters are, however, available the year round in Britain, as elsewhere. They are useful for cooked dishes and garnishes.

Canned oysters, both smoked and unsmoked are also available. Smoked oysters are best served alone or with other smoked fish, as an hors d'œuvre. Unsmoked ones can be useful in cooked dishes, although fewer should be used than when using fresh oysters as their flavour is somewhat insistent.

Oysters should be opened as near as possible to the time of eating. Do not try to open them yourself unless you are an expert. Ask your supplier either to loosen the shells or to open them completely, and to supply the deep shells as well as the oysters and their liquor in a container.

Serve oysters *au naturel* with thin slices of brown bread and butter, and quarters of lemon. You can also offer cayenne pepper, Tabasco sauce or vinegar separately.

PRAWNS, SHRIMPS AND SCAMPI

Prawns, shrimps and scampi are available all the year. Fresh ones are usually sold cooked; raw or cooked ones are also available in cans, and frozen.

To boil freshly caught prawns or shrimps Cooked prawns should be colourful and have no spawn when cooked; much depends on their freshness and the way in which they are cooked. Wash well, then put into boiling salted water and keep them boiling for about 7–8 min. Dublin Bay prawns will take rather longer, shrimps only 5 min. They are ready when they begin to change colour. Do not overboil or they will become tasteless and indigestible.

To shell prawns To shell prawns, take the head between the right-hand thumb and second finger, take the tip of the tail between the left thumb and forefinger, raise the shell at the knee or angle, pinch the tail and the shell will come apart, leaving the prawn attached to the head.

To shell shrimps Take the head between the right thumb and forefinger and with the left forefinger and thumbnail raise on each side the shell of the tail, pinch the tail, and the shell will at once separate.

'Scampi' is the Venetian name for very large prawns, similar to Dublin Bay prawns. They are now very popular as an hors d'œuvre or, grilled or sautéed, as a main-course dish. They are usually sold quick-frozen and uncooked, and must be cooked as soon as thawed. Ordinary boiled prawns are *not* suitable for most scampi recipes.

CREAMED SCAMPI

One 1-lb pkt small frozen scampi	$\frac{1}{2}$ pt thick white sauce
	2 tablesp single cream

Thaw the scampi sufficiently to separate them. Heat the sauce, add the cream and scampi and simmer for 4–5 min. Serve hot.

4 helpings

PREPARING SCALLOPS

Scallops are usually opened by the fishmonger and displayed in their flat shells. If the scallops are to be served in their shells ask the fishmonger for the *deep* shells. If, however, it is necessary to open scallops they should be put over a gentle heat to allow the shells to open. When they have opened, remove from the shells, trim away the beard and remove the black parts. Wash the scallops well, drain and dry. Wash and dry the shells; keep the deep shells for serving-dishes. Scallops are in season from November to March. They can be served baked, fried, poached or grilled.

Meat Dishes

ROASTED AND GRILLED MEATS

ROAST BEEF

Joint of beef
suitable for
roasting
Salt and pepper
Beef dripping
(allow 1 oz per
lb of meat)

Weigh meat to be able to calculate cooking time. Wipe with a damp cloth. Place joint in a roasting tin, season and add dripping. Put roasting tin into a very hot oven (230 °C, 450 °F, Gas 8) for 10–15 min to brown or 'sear' the meat. Then reduce heat to fairly hot (190 °C, 375 °F, Gas 5) and baste every 20 min for the first half of the cooking time and afterwards every 30 min. Allow 20 min per lb and another 10 min over for solid joints, i.e. joints without bone; and 15 min per lb and 15 min over for thick joints, i.e. joints with bone. Remove on to a hot dish when cooked, remove string and skewer with a metal skewer if necessary. Keep hot. Drain off fat from tin and make gravy from sediment in the tin. Yorkshire Pudding is roast beef's traditional companion, as is Horseradish Sauce.

YORKSHIRE OR BATTER PUDDING

$\frac{1}{2}$ **lb plain flour**
$\frac{1}{4}$ **teasp salt**
2 eggs
1 pt milk
1 tablesp cooking
fat *or* **lard**

Sift the flour and salt into a basin. Make a well in the centre of the flour and break the eggs into this. Add about a gill of the milk. Stir, gradually working the flour down from the sides and adding more milk, as required, to make a stiff batter consistency. Beat well for about 5 min. Add the rest of the milk. Cover and leave to stand for 30 min. Put the fat into a Yorkshire-pudding tin and heat in the oven until hot. The fat should just be beginning to smoke. Quickly pour in the batter and leave to cook in a hot oven (220 °C, 425 °F, Gas 7) at the top of the oven until nicely browned. Reduce the heat to 190 °C, 375 °F, Gas 5, and finish cooking through for 10–15 min.

6 helpings
Time (Large pudding)—35–40 min
       (Individual puddings)—20–25 min

GRILLED STEAK

$1\frac{1}{2}$ lb rump or fillet steak for sirloin	Maître d'Hôtel butter
Oil or butter	Watercress
Salt and pepper	(optional)

Wipe and cut the meat across the grain into suitable slices if required. Beat on both sides with a cutlet bat or rolling-pin if wanted thin.

Brush the slices with oil or melted butter and sprinkle with salt and pepper. Place under a red-hot grill, and grill quickly on both sides to seal the surfaces, thus preventing the juices from escaping. Then grill more slowly until cooked as you wish. A 'rare' steak is sealed only, remaining red inside. A 'medium' steak is still slightly pink inside, a 'well-done' steak is fully cooked through. The heat of the grill and the thickness of the steak will determine how long to cook each type. While cooking, turn the steaks frequently, using tongs or 2 spoons. Never pierce them with a fork as this makes holes through which the meat juices escape. Serve steaks at once with a pat of Maître d'Hôtel butter on top, and with watercress if available.

6 helpings

CHÂTEAUBRIAND STEAK

A double fillet steak not less than $1\frac{1}{2}$ in thick	Olive oil *or* melted butter
	Salt and pepper

Wipe the steak. Remove any sinew or skin. Cover the meat with a cloth and beat lightly to flatten. Brush over with oil or melted butter and season. Place under a red-hot grill and cook both sides quickly; the steak should be well browned but slightly underdone. Serve immediately on a hot dish with potato straws. Serve also Maître d'Hôtel butter and gravy.

CROWN ROAST OF LAMB WITH SAFFRON RICE

A 2-section crown roast of lamb	Salt
Oil for brushing	Pepper

Crown roast of lamb stuffed with saffron rice

Châteaubriand steak

45

Stuffing

1 oz butter	2 oz frozen peas
1 stick celery, chopped	1 oz chopped, blanched almonds
1 onion, chopped	2 dessert apples, cored and diced
5 oz long-grain white rice	1 oz butter
$\frac{1}{2}$ gill dry white wine	
1 pt chicken stock, heated, with a scant $\frac{1}{4}$ teasp powdered saffron	

Ask the butcher to prepare the crown roast. Place the joint in a roasting tin. Brush with oil and season well with salt and pepper. Wrap a small piece of foil around the top of each rib to prevent it from scorching during cooking. Cook at 190 °C, 375 °F, Gas 5, for $1\frac{1}{4}$–$1\frac{1}{2}$ hr. Approx 30 min before the joint is due to finish cooking, prepare the saffron rice stuffing by melting the butter in a saucepan and cooking the celery and onion until soft but not browned. Stir in the raw rice and cook for 1–2 min. Pour on the wine and cook gently until the rice has absorbed it. Add $\frac{1}{2}$ pt of the saffron-flavoured chicken stock and cook, uncovered, stirring occasionally, until almost all the liquid is absorbed. Pour the remaining stock over the rice and cook until it has been completely absorbed and the rice is just tender. Remove from the heat and add the peas, chopped nuts, diced apple and butter and cover the saucepan with fitting lid.

Drain the joint and place on a warmed serving-dish. Remove the foil from the rib bones. Fill the roast with the hot saffron rice. Top each rib with a cutlet frill and serve. (Any extra rice can be served separately.)

6–8 helpings

ROAST LEG OF LAMB

A small leg of lamb (boned)	1 shallot
1 carrot	1 clove of bruised garlic
1 onion	Salt and pepper
1 teasp chopped parsley	2 oz good dripping

Slice the carrot and onion and chop the shallot finely. Mix together the parsley, shallot, garlic, salt and pepper, and then sprinkle the mixture on the inner surface of the meat. Bind into a good shape. Place in a covered baking tin with the dripping, onion and carrot. Season well with salt and pepper. Bake for 20 min in a fairly hot oven (200 °C, 400 °F, Gas 6) then reduce heat to moderate (180 °C, 350 °F, Gas 4) for the remainder of the time, allowing 20 min per lb and 20 min over. For the last 10 min remove the covering and allow the meat to brown and become crisp. Serve on a hot dish with gravy made from the bones and the sediment in the baking tin, and with mint sauce if liked.

6–8 helpings

GRILLED LAMB OR PORK CUTLETS OR CHOPS

6–8 cutlets or chops	Salt and pepper Salad oil

Trim the cutlets or chops to a neat uniform shape. Season with salt and pepper and brush all over with salad oil. Grill, turning 3 or 4 times for about 8 min for cutlets, longer for chops, according to their thickness.

6–8 helpings
Cooking time about 10 min

MUTTON OR LAMB KEBABS

6 neat pieces of lamb or mutton, cut from leg	6 small mushrooms
3 small sliced onions	6 small tomatoes
	Oil or melted butter
6 thick bacon rashers	12 bay leaves

Trim the meat into neat even-shaped cubes. Cut the bacon in squares, and slice the tomatoes. Brush all (including tomatoes) with oil or butter and thread on to 6 skewers, interleaving with bay leaves. Grill for 10–15 min, turning as required. Serve on their skewers and if liked on a bed of risotto (rice cooked in stock in a casserole until stock is absorbed).

6 helpings

ROAST LOIN OF PORK WITH APPLE SAUCE

3 lb loin of pork	Apple sauce
1 tablesp finely	Brown gravy
chopped onion	
$\frac{1}{2}$ teasp powdered	
sage	
$\frac{1}{2}$ teasp salt	
1 saltsp dry	
mustard	
$\frac{1}{4}$ saltsp pepper	

Score the pork with narrow lines. Mix the onion with the sage, salt, mustard and pepper and rub the mixture well into the meat. Wrap the joint in greased greaseproof paper and roast in a covered tin in a hot oven (220 °C, 425 °F, Gas 7) for 10 min and then reduce heat to moderate (180 °C, 350 °F, Gas 4) for the remainder of the time. Allow 25 min per lb and 25 min over. About $\frac{1}{2}$ hr before serving, remove the paper and lid and continue cooking to crisp the crackling. Serve the apple sauce and gravy separately. Roast pork is also good served cold with salad.

6 helpings

BAKED HAM

A ham	Brown sugar
Flour	Cloves

Soak the ham in water for at least 12 hr. Wipe well and trim off any rusty bits. Coat with a flour and water paste crust which must be sufficiently thick all over to keep in the gravy. Place the ham in a fairly hot oven (200 °C, 400 °F, Gas 6) for about 15 min, then reduce heat to cool (150 °C, 310 °F, Gas 2) and cook for the remainder of the time allowing 30 min per lb. Remove the crust and skin, score squares in the fat and place a clove in each square, sprinkle brown sugar over the fat.

Glaze the sugar by placing the ham in a fierce oven (230 °C, 450 °F, Gas 8) for a few minutes or under a hot grill. Garnish the knuckle with a paper frill before serving.

Small joints or pieces of ham or gammon can be cooked in the same way; obviously they take less time.

GAMMON STEAKS WITH RICE

$\frac{1}{2}$ lb rice	2 eating apples,
2 tablesp chopped	cored and
parsley	chopped
Seasoning	6 oz grated cheese
2 oz butter	4 thick gammon
3 oz white	steaks
breadcrumbs	Parsley

Cook the rice in boiling salted water until tender. Drain, stir in the chopped parsley and seasoning, and keep warm. Grill the gammon steaks, turning them once. While they grill, sauté the breadcrumbs in butter, add the diced apple and cook for 2–3 min. Remove from the heat and stir in half the grated cheese.

Place rice in a serving-dish, arrange the gammon steaks overlapping, with apple-crumb mixture between each slice, sprinkle with grated cheese and replace under the hot grill for a moment or two. Garnish with parsley.

4 helpings

ESCALOPES OF VEAL, VIENNESE STYLE

$1\frac{1}{4}$–$1\frac{1}{2}$ lb fillet of	Egg and
veal cut in 6	breadcrumbs
slices	Oil *or* butter for
Salt and pepper	frying
Flour	Lemon juice

Noisette butter

2 oz butter	Cayenne pepper
Salt and pepper	

Garnish

6 stoned olives	1 tablesp chopped
6 boned anchovy	parsley
fillets	Slices of lemon
1 hard-boiled egg	

Wipe the meat, season, dip in flour and coat with egg and breadcrumbs. Heat the oil or butter and fry the escalopes for about 5 min until golden-brown. Make the noisette butter by heating the butter in a saucepan until golden-brown, then seasoning with salt, pepper and cayenne. Place the escalopes slightly overlapping on a hot dish. Sprinkle with lemon juice and pour over the noisette butter. Garnish with olives wrapped in anchovy fillets. Place the chopped egg white, sieved egg yolk and chopped parsley at either end of the dish. Serve with lemon slices.

6 helpings

Roast loin of pork with apple sauce

Loin of veal, daube style

BRAISED BOILED AND REHEATED MEAT DISHES

BRAISED BEEF WITH PEPPERS

2 lb topside *or* brisket of beef	1 oz dripping
1 large carrot	Bouquet garni
1 large turnip	6–12 peppercorns
18 button onions	Salt
2 leeks	Stock
A few sticks of celery	3 green *or* red peppers
$\frac{1}{4}$ lb fat bacon rashers	Black olives (optional)

Wipe and trim the meat and tie into a good shape. Dice the carrot and turnip. Fry vegetables lightly in a pan with the bacon rinds in hot dripping. Place the meat on top and cover with slices of bacon. Add the bouquet garni and peppercorns tied in muslin, salt to taste and enough stock to nearly cover the vegetables. Cover with a well-fitting lid and cook as slowly as possible for about 3 hr, basting occasionally and adding more stock if necessary. When nearly ready, chop and cook the peppers for a few min in well-flavoured stock. Make a clear brown gravy, adding any strained stock left in the stewpan. Place the meat on a hot dish, remove string and carve in slices. Garnish with onions and peppers, and the stoned olives, if used. Pour over the gravy.

6–8 helpings

BEEF OLIVES

$1\frac{1}{2}$ lb stewing steak	Salt and pepper to taste
2 oz fresh white breadcrumbs	1 egg
	1 oz plain flour
1 rounded tablesp dried skim milk powder	2 oz dripping
	$\frac{1}{2}$ lb onions, peeled and sliced
4 level tablesp chopped suet	1 pt stock
2 level tablesp chopped parsley	1 pt pkt dehydrated 'instant' potato
A good pinch of dried herbs	$\frac{1}{2}$ teasp ground nutmeg
Grated rind of $\frac{1}{2}$ lemon	

Remove any excess fat from the meat and cut it into 12 even-sized pieces. For the stuffing, mix together the breadcrumbs, dry milk powder, suet, parsley, herbs, lemon rind and seasoning. Stir in the egg with a little more milk powder made into liquid if necessary. Use just enough to bind the mixture lightly together. Divide the stuffing between the pieces of meat and roll into neat rolls. Wind a piece of cotton round the meat or use a wooden cocktail skewer, to keep the stuffing in place. Add a little seasoning to the flour and roll the meat in it. Heat the dripping in a heat-proof casserole or pan and fry the meat until browned all over. Carefully lift out the meat. Fry the onions and carrots until lightly browned, then return the meat to the casserole, with any remaining flour. Pour over the stock and bring slowly to the boil. Put a lid on the pan or casserole and simmer for about $1\frac{1}{2}$ hr until the meat is tender. The beef olives can also be cooked in a slow oven (150 °C, 310 °F, Gas 2), for about $2\frac{1}{2}$ hr.

6 helpings

BRAISED LEG OR SHOULDER OF LAMB

A large leg *or* shoulder of lamb	Bouquet garni
2 onions	10 peppercorns
1 turnip	2 shallots
2 carrots	$1\frac{1}{2}$ oz butter
1 oz dripping	$1\frac{1}{2}$ oz flour
Stock	Salt and pepper

Thickly slice the onions, turnip and carrots. Melt the dripping in a saucepan and sweat the sliced vegetables in it with the lid on, over a gentle heat for 5–10 min. Almost cover with stock or water, add the bouquet garni and peppercorns. Place the prepared meat on top, put a piece of greased greaseproof paper on top of the pan and cover with a good-fitting lid. Cook gently for $3-3\frac{1}{2}$ hr, basting occasionally with the stock and adding more stock if necessary. About $\frac{1}{2}$ hr before serving, chop the shallots very finely, melt the butter and fry the shallots lightly. Then add the flour and cook until a good brown colour. Keep the meat hot, strain the stock and make up to 1 pt. Add the stock to the browned flour and butter and stir until boiling. Season to taste and pour a little over the meat. Serve the remainder in a sauceboat. If preferred, the meat can be boned and the cavity filled with a stuffing made as follows: equal quantities of ham and trimmings from the leg finely chopped, finely chopped onion and a little garlic if liked. Allow an extra $\frac{1}{2}$ hr for cooking. Either way, serve with plainly dished vegetables flavoured with a mild herb rather than with fat.

8–12 helpings

LANCASHIRE HOT POT

2 lb best end of	Salt and pepper
neck of lamb	Stock
2 lb potatoes	1 oz butter *or*
3 sheep's kidneys	margarine
1 large onion	$\frac{1}{2}$ pt thin gravy

Divide the meat into neat cutlets. Trim off the skin and most of the fat. Grease a fireproof baking dish and put in a layer of sliced potatoes. Arrange the cutlets on top, slightly overlapping each other, and cover with slices of kidneys and slices of onion. Season well. Add the remainder of the potatoes. The top layer should be of small potatoes cut in halves, uniformly arranged to give a neat appearance to the dish. Pour down the side of the dish about $\frac{1}{2}$ pt hot stock seasoned with salt and pepper. Brush the top layer of potatoes with warmed fat and cover with greased greaseproof paper. Bake for about 2 hr in a moderate oven (180 °C, 350 °F, Gas 4). Then remove the paper to allow the potatoes to become crisp and brown, cooking for a further 20 min. When ready to serve; pour some gravy down the sides of the dish and serve the rest in a gravy-boat. Serve the hot pot in the dish in which it is cooked.

6 helpings

NAVARIN OF LAMB

1 large breast *or*	Bouquet garni
boned neck of	8–10 small onions
lamb	8–10 small
A good pinch of	potatoes
sugar	10 oz peas, frozen,
1 large tablesp	dehydrated *or*
flour	canned (optional)
$\frac{1}{2}$ lb skinned	10 oz small whole
tomatoes	carrots, frozen *or*
1 crushed clove of	canned (optional)
garlic	Chopped parsley
Salt and pepper	

Cut the lamb in neat slices, having trimmed off tag ends and excess fat. Chop the fat and heat it gently. Fry the meat pieces in some of it, then transfer them to a casserole. Pour off the fat. Sprinkle the sugar into the pan and heat until it becomes a deep gold. Work in the flour and then the chopped tomatoes (seeds discarded), then stir in enough hot water to make a sauce to cover the meat. Pour over the meat. Add the crushed garlic, a little pepper and salt and the bouquet garni. Cover, cook for $1\frac{1}{2}$ hr first in a moderate oven (180 °C, 350 °F, Gas 4) reducing to 150 °C, 310 °F, Gas 2 after $\frac{1}{2}$ hr. Remove bouquet garni; add the onions and potatoes, turn up the heat to 180 °C, 350 °F, Gas 4 and cook for a further $\frac{1}{2}-\frac{3}{4}$ hr. Add the drained, cooked peas and carrots if used, and heat through. Sprinkle with parsley and serve.

6 helpings

BRAISED PORK CHOPS IN CIDER

4 pork chops	2–3 large dark
4 tablesp cider	mushrooms
Bouquet garni	1 breakfastcup *or*
3 onions	10-oz can garden
2 cooking apples	peas
Good pinch of	1 breakfastcup *or*
ground cinnamon	10-oz can
Salt and pepper	beetroots
	6–8 oz noodles

Trim off rind and excessive fat and quickly fry chops in them until golden-brown. Place in a casserole, add cider and bouquet garni, cover and cook gently on the cooker or in a

Lancashire hot pot

left: Grilled and sautéed kidneys

far right: Corned beef pie

cool oven (150°–170°C, 310°–335°F, Gas
2–3). Meanwhile, pour off excess fat from
frying-pan; peel, chop, then fry the onions
and apples for a few minutes. Add the cinnamon and water to cover them, put on a lid
and simmer until soft. Sieve, season to taste
and turn on to the chops. Cover and cook for
$1\frac{3}{4}$–2 hr in all, adding the thickly sliced
mushrooms $\frac{1}{2}$ hr before the end. Heat the
peas and beetroots separately. Trickle the
noodles into salted boiling water and boil
until, on testing a piece, the centre is still
slightly firm (about 8 min). Drain the
noodles, peas and beetroots. Dish the noodles
with the chops on top and garnish with the
mushrooms, peas and beetroots.

4 helpings

52

LOIN OF VEAL, DAUBE STYLE

A small shoulder of veal	1 turnip
Salt and pepper	2 stalks celery
2 oz dripping	Bouquet garni
2 onions	Stock as required
	Piquant sauce

Stuffing

½ large onion	Parsley
1 oz butter	2 egg yolks
3 stalks celery	3–4 oz white
2 eating apples	breadcrumbs
1 oz walnuts, chopped	Stock

Bone the veal, flatten it out and season well with salt and pepper. Roll up and tie with string. Sauté in hot fat until brown on all sides and remove. Peel the onions, carrots, turnips; clean the celery, chop coarsely; fry all the vegetables in dripping until just turning colour. Make a mound of the sautéed vegetables in centre of casserole. Place veal on top, add the bouquet garni and sufficient stock to cover the vegetables and braise with lid on until meat is tender.

Stuffing

Peel and slice the onion; fry in butter until soft. Add the finely diced celery and apples, walnuts and parsley and egg yolks and sufficient breadcrumbs to make a soft stuffing. Simmer, moistening with stock when necessary, for 15 min.

Serve veal on a bed of the vegetables with the stuffing arranged at each end of the veal, and serve Piquant sauce separately.

BOILED BEEF, FRESH OR SALTED

2½–3 lb unsalted silverside, aitchbone *or* round of beef *or* brisket	10 peppercorns
	A bunch of herbs
	Carrots
Salt	Turnips
3 cloves	Onions
	Suet dumplings

Wipe the meat with a damp cloth and tie into a neat shape with string. Put into a pan and cover with boiling salted water. Bring to the boil again and boil for 5 min to seal the surface. Reduce to simmering point, add the cloves, peppercorns and herbs and simmer for the remainder of the time, allowing 20 min per lb and 20 min over. Skim when necessary. Add the sliced vegetables allowing enough time for them to be cooked when the meat is ready. Place the meat on a hot dish. Remove string and re-skewer meat if necessary. Arrange vegetables neatly round and serve some of the liquid separately in a sauceboat.

If suet dumplings are to be served, put them into the liquor $\frac{1}{2}$ hr before serving.

In boiling meat a certain proportion of the nutritive qualities escape into the water; the liquor therefore should be utilized for soup, when it is not too salty for the purpose. With this end in view the liquor should be reduced to the smallest possible quantity by using a pan just large enough to contain the joint, with barely sufficient water to cover.

EXETER STEW

$1\frac{1}{2}$ lb lean beef	$1\frac{1}{2}$ oz flour
$1\frac{1}{2}$ oz dripping	1 teasp vinegar
3 medium-sized onions	Salt and pepper

Savoury dumplings

4 oz flour	$\frac{1}{2}$ teasp mixed herbs
$\frac{1}{4}$ teasp baking powder	1 teasp salt
$1\frac{1}{2}$ oz finely chopped suet	$\frac{1}{2}$ teasp pepper
1 tablesp finely-chopped parsley	Egg *or* milk

Wipe the meat and remove all the fat. Cut the meat into pieces about 2 in by $2\frac{1}{2}$ in. Heat the fat in a stewpan until smoking hot and fry the meat until brown. Remove the meat and fry the sliced onions. Then add the flour and cook, stirring until brown. Add $1\frac{1}{4}$ pt water and bring to the boil, stirring constantly. Simmer for a few minutes. Add the vinegar and seasoning, return the meat and simmer gently for about 2 hr. Mix the ingredients for the savoury dumplings together, bind with the egg or milk into a stiff mixture and make into 12 balls. Bring the stew to boiling point about 30 min before time for serving and drop in the dumplings.

Simmer for the remainder of the time. Pile the meat in the centre of a hot dish, pour the gravy over and arrange the dumplings neatly round the base.

6 helpings

GOULASH OF BEEF

$1\frac{1}{2}$ lb lean beef	2 tomatoes
2 oz dripping	Salt
2 onions	Paprika
$1\frac{1}{2}$ oz flour	Bouquet garni
1 pt stock	6 diced potatoes
$\frac{1}{4}$ pt red wine (optional)	2 tablesp sour cream (optional)

Wipe and trim the meat, removing any skin and fat. Cut into neat pieces. Heat the fat and sauté the sliced onions with the meat, until the meat is evenly browned. Add the flour and stir until brown. Then add the stock, wine, skinned and diced tomatoes, salt, paprika and bouquet garni. Stir, bring to the boil. If liked, transfer to a casserole and cook slowly for $1\frac{1}{2}$–2 hr in the oven, stirring occasionally, or continue cooking in saucepan for the same time. Add the diced potatoes about $\frac{1}{2}$ hr before the goulash is ready. They should be cooked but not broken. 2 tablesp sour cream may be stirred in before serving or used to top the individual servings.

6 helpings

BOILED LEG OF LAMB OR MUTTON

A small leg of well-aged lamb *or* mutton	$\frac{1}{2}$ teasp mixed herbs
2 tablesp breadcrumbs	Salt and pepper
	A little milk
1 tablesp finely chopped suet	Stock *or* water with vegetables,
1 dessertsp chopped parsley	10 peppercorns, and salt

Remove all bone and surplus fat; season well. Make the stuffing by mixing the breadcrumbs, suet, parsley, herbs, salt and pepper together. Moisten with milk. Spread the mixture on the meat, re-form its shape and bind securely with string. Put into the boiling stock or water and stock vegetables, and simmer for 2–3 hr, according to size. Pour caper sauce over the meat, if liked.

Leg and neck of mutton can be cooked in the same way.

6–8 helpings

HARICOT MUTTON

6 small chops from the middle neck *or* 2 lb scrag end 1 oz butter *or* good dripping	1 large onion 1 oz flour 1½ pt stock Salt and pepper Bouquet garni

Trim off the skin and surplus fat and cut the meat into small pieces or cutlets. Put the butter or dripping into a saucepan and when smoking, fry the meat quickly and lightly. Remove the meat, chop the onion finely and fry slowly in the same fat without browning. Add the flour and fry slowly until a rich brown. Cool slightly and add the stock, seasoning and bouquet garni. Bring to the boil, put in the meat and simmer gently until tender—about 2 hr. Cut the carrots and turnip into neat dice for garnish. Add the rough trimmings to the meat. Cook the diced carrot and turnip separately in boiling salted water until just tender. Arrange the meat on a hot dish. If necessary rapidly boil the liquid in the saucepan to reduce and then strain over the meat. Garnish with the diced carrot and turnip.

6 helpings

IRISH STEW

2 lb best end of neck of lamb 1 lb onions Salt and pepper	3 lb potatoes 1½ pt stock *or* water Parsley

Cut the meat into neat pieces and trim off the surplus fat. Arrange in a saucepan layers of the meat, thinly sliced onions, seasoning and ½ the potatoes cut in slices. Add stock or water just to cover and simmer gently for about 1½ hr. Add the rest of the potatoes, cut to a uniform size to improve the appearance on top. Cook gently in the steam for about ¾ hr longer. Serve the meat in the centre of a hot dish and arrange the potatoes round the edge. Pour the liquid over the

meat and sprinkle with finely chopped parsley.

An alternative method of serving is to place the meat in the centre of a hot dish. Arrange ½ the potatoes round the edge. Then sieve the liquid, onions and remaining potatoes, or process in an electric blender. Pour over the meat. Sprinkle with chopped parsley.

6 helpings

BOILED PICKLED PORK OR BACON WITH BEANS

A joint of pickled *or* salt pork *or* bacon forehock Broad beans *or* dried butter beans	10 peppercorns 1 carrot 1 onion ½ turnip Salt Parsley sauce

Soak the beans overnight. Soak the meat in cold water. Cover the pork with fresh cold water and simmer gently, allowing 25–30 min per lb and 25–30 min over. When the liquid is boiling, add the peppercorns, and the carrot, onion and turnip cut in thick slices. Also add the beans, if dried. About ½ hr before the pork is cooked, cook fresh beans in boiling salted water, simmer gently until tender but whole. Drain well and coat with parsley sauce. Pease pudding or peas may be served in place of the beans if liked. Serve the pork in a hot dish, garnished with the vegetables. The liquor in which the pork is cooked can be made into good pea soup.

BOILED HAM OR BACON

1 ham *or* large smoked bacon joint such as forehock Meat glaze *or* raspings	Brown sugar (to use with raspings) Cumberland sauce

Soak the ham or bacon well for 12 hr if very salty and dry. Clean and trim off any rusty parts. Lay the soaked meat on a cloth in a big pan, cover with fresh water and simmer until cooked, allowing 20–30 min per lb. When cooked, remove from the water, strip off the skin. If to be eaten cold, replace the joint in the water until cool, to keep it moist.

Beef olives

Irish stew

Before serving, sprinkle with raspings and sugar, or meat glaze. Serve hot with Cumberland sauce or cold with fruit (*see* Bacon with Fruit).

BLANQUETTE OF LAMB OR VEAL

2 lb fleshy lamb-loin, neck *or* **breast** *or* **veal, taken from the shoulder**	**2 tablesp cream** *or* **dried skim milk powder made up double strength**
Salt and pepper	
1 large onion	
Bouquet garni	
6 peppercorns	
Pinch of grated nutmeg	
Stock *or* **water**	
1½ oz butter	
1 oz flour	
1 egg yolk	

Garnish

Croûtes of fried bread *or* **fleurons of pastry**	**Button mushrooms**

Cut the meat into pieces about 2 in square and put into a stewpan with salt, sliced onion, herbs, peppercorns and nutmeg. Just cover with cold stock or water and simmer until tender—about 2 hr. When the meat is cooked, melt the butter in a saucepan and stir in the flour. Cook for a few minutes without browning. Strain ½ pt liquor from the meat and add to the blended flour and butter. Stir until boiling then simmer for 3 min. Beat together the egg yolk and cream or milk and add to the sauce. Stir and cook gently for a few minutes; do not allow to boil or it may curdle. Correct the seasoning. Arrange the meat on a hot dish, piling it high in the centre and strain the sauce over. Garnish with neatly shaped croûtes of fried bread or fleurons of pastry and grilled mushrooms. Serve hot.

5–6 helpings

56

Boiled gammon with Cumberland sauce

Blanquette of veal

BEEF, LAMB OR MUTTON HASH

$1\frac{1}{2}$ lb cooked
beef, lamb or
mutton (approx)
Breadcrumbs
Gherkins
Salt and pepper
$\frac{3}{4}$ pt brown sauce

Cut the meat into neat slices. Grease a 1 pt pie-dish and sprinkle with breadcrumbs. Arrange a layer of slices of meat slightly overlapping each other. Sprinkle with finely chopped gherkins, salt and pepper and 2–3 tablesp brown sauce. Repeat until all ingredients are used, making the top layer a rather thicker one of breadcrumbs. Cover with greaseproof paper and bake gently, for about $\frac{1}{2}$ hr in a moderate oven (180 °C, 350 °F, Gas 4). Serve in the pie-dish.

6 helpings

RÉCHAUFFÉ OF LAMB

$1\frac{1}{2}$ lb cold cooked
lamb
1 small onion
$\frac{3}{4}$ oz butter or
margarine
$\frac{1}{2}$ oz flour
$\frac{3}{4}$ pt gravy or
stock
1 tablesp
mushroom
ketchup

Salt and pepper
Mashed potatoes
or boiled rice

Cut the meat into neat dice and boil the bones and trimmings for stock. Finely chop the onion, melt the fat in a saucepan and fry the onion lightly. Add the flour and brown. Stir in the stock, add the ketchup and season to taste. Simmer for 10 min. Put in the meat and bring to simmering point. Keep just below simmering for about $\frac{1}{2}$ hr. Serve the meat surrounded by a border of mashed potatoes or boiled rice.

6 helpings

SHEPHERD'S PIE

1 lb cold cooked beef *or* mutton	2 lb cooked mashed potatoes
1 small onion	Egg *or* milk
$\frac{1}{2}$ pt gravy	Salt and pepper

Remove any skin, gristle or bone and cut the meat into small dice. Parboil and finely chop the onion and place in a pie-dish with the meat and the gravy. Season well. Cover with mashed potatoes and smooth and decorate the top to look like pie-crust. Glaze with beaten egg or milk if liked. Bake in a moderate oven (180 °C, 350 °F, Gas 4) for about $\frac{1}{2}$ hr until thoroughly warmed and the surface is well browned.

Shepherd's Pie can be made in individual dishes if you prefer.

6 helpings

TOAD IN THE HOLE

4 oz plain flour	1 lb skinless sausages *or* sausage meat
$\frac{1}{4}$ teasp salt	
1 egg	
$\frac{1}{2}$ pt milk *or* milk and water	1 tablesp cooking fat *or* dripping

Make a batter with the flour, salt, egg and milk, and leave to stand for $\frac{1}{2}$ hr. Heat the fat in a Yorkshire-pudding tin, put the sausages or rolls of sausage meat in the hot fat, pour the batter over and bake in a hot oven (220 °C, 425 °F, Gas 7) for about 30 min.

STEAK OR STEAK AND KIDNEY PIE

$1\frac{1}{2}$ lb lean beefsteak	Flaky, puff *or* short crust pastry, using 8 oz flour, etc.
Seasoned flour	
2 onions	
Stock *or* water	Egg *or* milk

Wipe the meat, remove the skin and superfluous fat and cut meat into small cubes. Dip the cubes in the seasoned flour and place in a pie-dish, piling them higher in the centre. Peel and finely chop the onions; sprinkle any remaining seasoned flour between the meat. Add enough stock or water to $\frac{1}{4}$ fill the dish. Roll out the pastry $\frac{1}{4}-\frac{1}{2}$ in thick to the shape of the pie-dish, but allow an extra 2 in all round. Cut a strip about $\frac{3}{4}$ in wide from around the edge of the pastry to cover the rim of the pie-dish. Dampen the rim, place the strip of pastry around with the cut side out and allow it to overlap the rim a little. Damp the join and the rest of the pastry and cover with the pastry lid. Press the edges lightly together. Trim, make a small round hole in the centre of the pie, and decorate with pastry leaves. Brush with beaten egg or milk. Place in a hot oven (230 °C, 450 °F, Gas 8) until pastry is set and then reduce heat; if necessary place the pie on a lower shelf and cover with greased paper to prevent pastry becoming too brown. Heat the stock. Use the hole in the pie to pour in the hot stock before serving.

For Steak and Kidney Pie add 2 sheep's or 6 oz ox kidneys. Soak the kidneys, remove the skins and cores and cut into slices or quarters. Then add to the pie meat. Prepare and cook as described above.

6 helpings   Cooking time about 2 hr

MEAT PIES AND PUDDINGS

STEAK OR STEAK AND KIDNEY PUDDING

$1\frac{1}{2}$ lb good stewing steak	3 tablesp stock *or* water (approx)
Seasoned flour	
Suet crust pastry, using 8 oz flour, etc.	

Wipe the meat; remove any superfluous skin and fat. Cut the meat into narrow strips or cubes and dip in the seasoned flour. Cut off $\frac{1}{3}$ of the pastry for the lid. Roll the remainder out into a round about $\frac{1}{4}$ in thick and line a greased pudding basin with it. Press well in to remove any creases. Half-fill the basin with the prepared meat and add the stock or water. Then add the remainder of the meat. Roll out the pastry reserved for the lid. Damp the edges, place the lid on top and press the edges well together. Cover with greased foil or greaseproof paper if pudding is to be steamed, or with a pudding cloth if it is to be boiled. Place in boiling water and steam for about $3\frac{1}{2}$ hr—keep the water boiling, if necessary add more *boiling* water; *or* boil for 3 hr. Serve in the pudding basin, or turn out on to a hot dish.

To make a Steak and Kidney Pudding add to the meat 2 sheep's or 6 oz of ox kidney. Soak the kidneys, remove the skins and cores and cut into slices or quarters. Dip in seasoned flour, place in the basin and proceed as described above for Beefsteak Pudding.

6 helpings

PORK AND ONION DUMPLING

1 lb lean pork	Salt and pepper
3 onions	Pinch of sage
Suet crust pastry using 12 oz flour, etc.	

Chop the pork; finely chop the onions. Roll out the suet crust pastry in a neat rectangle. On it place the pork, seasoning, sage and onion, leaving a margin all round. Roll up, securing the edges firmly. Wrap firmly in several layers of buttered greaseproof paper and secure safely. Steam for 3 hr and serve with a good brown gravy.

6 helpings

CORNED BEEF PIE

Rich short crust pastry, using 8 oz flour, 4 oz lard, 1 egg yolk, etc. (no sugar)	2 tablesp chopped parsley Stock Salt and pepper

Filling

1 12-oz can corned beef	1 tablesp Worcester sauce
1 oz butter	3 oz button mushrooms, peeled and sliced
2 medium onions, peeled and chopped	

Topping

2 egg whites, stiffly beaten	2 oz finely grated Cheddar cheese
2 oz finely grated Parmesan cheese	

Make a flan case with the pastry, and bake it 'blind'. Mash the corned beef. Melt the butter and sauté the onions for 10 min. Stir in the meat, Worcester sauce, mushrooms and parsley. Cover and simmer for 20 min, moistening with stock when necessary. Season with salt and pepper and turn into the baked flan case. Fold the cheeses into egg whites and pile on top of the pie. Place in a hot oven (230 °C, 450 °F, Gas 7–8) until golden and serve hot.

POT PIE OF VEAL

$1\frac{1}{4}$ lb lean veal	1 lb potatoes
$\frac{1}{2}$ lb pickled pork	Puff pastry using 6 oz flour, etc.
Salt and pepper Stock	

Cut the meat into pieces convenient for serving and cut the pork into thin small slices. Place the meat and pork in layers in a large pie-dish, seasoning each layer well with salt and pepper, and fill the dish $\frac{3}{4}$ full with stock. Cover with a lid and cook in a moderate oven (180 °C, 350 °F, Gas 4) for $1\frac{1}{2}$ hr. Meanwhile parboil the potatoes and cut in thick slices. After cooking for $1\frac{1}{2}$ hr, allow the meat to cool slightly. Add more stock if necessary, place the potatoes on top, cover with pastry and make a hole in the top. Bake in a very hot oven (230 °C, 450 °F, Gas 8) until the pastry is set, reduce heat and cook more slowly for the remainder of the time, making 40–50 min altogether. Add more hot stock through the hole in the top before serving. Garnish with parsley and serve.

6 helpings

top left: Shepherd's pies

left: Boiled pickled pork with broad beans

top right: Gammon steaks with rice

bottom right: Baked ox liver

OFFAL DISHES

CASSEROLED LAMBS' HEARTS

6 lambs' hearts	**2 oz dripping**
Veal forcemeat	**$\frac{1}{2}$ pt good stock**
or **mixed chopped**	**$\frac{3}{4}$ oz flour**
parsley and	**Salt and pepper**
butter *or* **minced**	
bacon	

Soak the hearts for about $\frac{1}{2}$ hr. Wash well in
clean water. Cut the pipes from the top,
leave the flaps to fasten down and cut the
dividing walls of the chambers. Dry
thoroughly and fill the hearts with forcemeat or parsley mixture, fold over the flaps
and tie or skewer to keep it in. Heat the
dripping in a casserole. Put in the hearts,
baste well and bake in a cool to moderate
oven (150°–180°C, 310°–350°F, Gas 2–4)
for $1\frac{1}{2}$ hr. When cooked, place the hearts on
a hot dish and keep hot. Drain off most of
the fat but keep back any sediment. Blend
the flour and stock and add to the sediment
to make thickened gravy. Season carefully.

61

Pour a little round the hearts and serve the rest in a gravy-boat.

6 helpings

GRILLED KIDNEYS

6 sheep's kidneys	**Croûtes of fried**
Oil *or* **oiled butter**	**bread**
Salt and pepper	

Garnish

Maître d'Hôtel butter

Prepare the kidneys as directed in the preceding recipe and keep them open and flat with a skewer. Brush with oil or melted butter and season with salt and pepper. Grill quickly, cooking the cut side first and turning frequently. When ready, remove the skewer and serve on croûtes of fried bread on a hot dish. The hollow in the centre of the kidney may be filled with a small pat of Maître d'Hôtel butter.

6 helpings

SAUTÉED KIDNEYS

6 sheep's kidneys	**Salt and pepper**
2 shallots	**Watercress**
1 oz butter *or* **fat**	**Croûtes of fried**
$\frac{1}{4}$ pt brown sauce	*or* **toasted bread**
1 tablesp sherry	

Skin the kidneys and remove the cores. Soak for 5 min in cold water. Dry and cut into $\frac{1}{4}$-in slices. Finely chop the shallots, heat the fat in a sauté pan and fry them slightly. Then put in the sliced kidney and shake and toss over the heat for about 5 min. Drain off the surplus fat and add the brown sauce, sherry (if used) and salt and pepper. Stir over a gentle heat until thoroughly hot, but take care not to let the mixture boil. Serve as hot as possible on toast or fried bread, garnished with watercress.

6 helpings

BAKED OX LIVER

1–1$\frac{1}{2}$ lb ox liver	**Seasoned flour**

$\frac{1}{4}$ lb fat bacon	**Parsley**
Stock *or* **water**	

Wash the liver in tepid salt water, remove any skin and tubes and cut the liver in thick slices. Place in a deep baking tin or dish. Lay the rashers of bacon on top and add enough stock or water to $\frac{1}{2}$ cover the liver. Cover the dish with foil or greaseproof paper, greased. Bake gently for 1$\frac{1}{2}$–2 hr, basting well and dredging frequently with seasoned flour. Remove the cover some 20 min before serving, to crisp the bacon somewhat. Dish neatly and strain the gravy round. Garnish with parsley.

OXTAIL STEW

2 ox tails	**Salt and pepper**
2 oz fat	**Bouquet garni**
2 onions	**Cloves to taste**
1$\frac{1}{2}$ oz flour	**Mace to taste**
1$\frac{1}{2}$ pt stock *or*	**Juice of $\frac{1}{2}$ lemon**
water	

Garnish

Croûtons of fried	**Dice** *or* **glazed**
bread	**strips of carrot**
	and turnip

Wash the tails, dry well and remove any superfluous fat. Cut into joints and divide the thick parts in half. Melt the fat in a saucepan, fry the pieces of tail until brown, then remove from the pan. Slice the onions and fry them until light brown, add the flour, mix well and fry slowly until a good brown colour. Add the stock or water, salt, pepper, bouquet garni, cloves and mace and bring to boiling point, stirring all the time. Return the pieces of tail and simmer gently for about 2$\frac{1}{2}$–3 hr. Remove the meat and arrange on a hot dish. Add the lemon juice to the sauce, correct the seasoning, strain and pour over the meat. Garnish with croûtons of fried bread and diced or thin strips of cooked carrot and turnip.

6 helpings

BOILED TONGUE

1 ox tongue	A bunch of
1 onion	mixed herbs
1 carrot	Parsley
1 turnip	

Wash the tongue thoroughly and soak for about 2 hr. If the tongue is dry and rather hard soak for 12 hr. If pickled, soak for about 3-4 hr. After soaking, put the tongue into a large pan of cold water, bring slowly to the boil, skim and add the onion, carrot, turnip and bunch of herbs. Cook gently, allowing 30 min per lb and 30 min over. When ready, lift out the tongue and remove the skin very carefully. Serve with parsley or caper sauce.

To serve cold After skin has been removed, shape tongue on a board by sticking a fork through the root and another through the top to straighten it. Leave until cold, trim and then glaze. Put a paper frill around the root and garnish with parsley.

Alternatively put the tongue in a bowl or tin, curling it round tightly, cover with stock, put a saucer on top and press with a weight on top. Leave until cold, then turn out.

BRAISED SWEETBREADS

2 oz lambs'	Seasoning
sweetbreads	1 bay leaf
$\frac{1}{2}$ oz butter	Pinch of herbs
$\frac{1}{2}$ oz flour	1 dessertsp sherry
$\frac{1}{4}$ pt good brown	
stock	

Put the washed sweetbreads into a pan of water. Bring to boil and simmer for 10-15 min. Drain off liquid, skin and chop sweetbreads. Heat butter in pan; stir in flour and cook for several minutes. Add stock. Bring to boil and cook until thickened. Add the sweetbreads, seasoning, bay leaf and herbs. Simmer for 10 min. Remove bay leaf, add sherry. Serve with creamed potatoes.

1 portion	Cooking time 25 min

TRIPE AND ONIONS

$1\frac{1}{2}$ lb tripe	2 large onions
$\frac{1}{2}$ pt milk	1 oz flour
1 teasp salt	Salt and pepper

Blanch the tripe, if not bought blanched and partly cooked, and cut into 3 in squares. Put in a saucepan with the milk, $\frac{1}{2}$ pt water and the salt; bring to the boil. Peel and slice the onions finely. Add them to the tripe and simmer very slowly for 2 hr. Mix the flour to a smooth paste with a little milk and add to the pan. Stir with a wooden spoon until boiling. Simmer for another 10 min, season to taste and serve.

6 helpings

COLD MEATS

BRAISED BEEF IN ASPIC

$1\frac{1}{2}$ lb fillet of beef	French mustard
previously	$1\frac{1}{4}$ pt aspic jelly
braised	Cooked peas
1 jar of meat	Cooked carrots
paste	

It is better to braise the beef the previous day if possible and allow it to become quite cold. Trim into an oblong shape and cut lengthwise into slices. Spread each slice alternately with meat paste and mustard, put the slices together again and press between 2 boards. Set a layer of aspic jelly at the bottom of a cake- or bread-tin and decorate with cooked peas and rings of cooked carrots. Pour on another layer of cold, liquid aspic jelly and allow it to set. Place the prepared beef on top, fill up the mould with aspic jelly and allow to set. Unmould on to an oval dish and decorate with chopped aspic. Serve with an appropriate salad or rice.

6 helpings

PRESSED BEEF

Salt brisket of	$\frac{1}{2}$ turnip
beef	Bouquet garni
1 onion	10 peppercorns
1 carrot	Meat glaze

continued on page 66

63

above left: Boiled beef with carrots and dumplings

below left: Bacon with fruit

Braised beef in aspic

Weigh the meat. Wash it well, or if very salt soak for about 1 hr in cold water. Put into cold water and bring slowly to boiling point. Skim well. Cut the prepared vegetables into large pieces, add to the meat with the bouquet garni and peppercorns, and simmer gently, allowing 25 min per lb and 25 min over. Take the meat out, remove the bones and press between 2 boards or dishes or roll and tie up. Leave until cold. Then brush over with meat glaze.

BACON WITH FRUIT

1 small joint of bacon	A few cloves
Brown sugar	1 small bunch grapes
3 pears, peeled, cored and halved, dipped in lemon juice	2 small oranges, cut into wedges

Soak the bacon overnight, then boil it (*see* Boiled Ham). Remove from water and cool. Press brown sugar around the sides. Decorate the pear halves with the cloves and place these, the grapes and the orange wedges around the ham.

PORK PIE

1 lb lean pork	$\frac{1}{2}$ gill water *or* stock
Powdered herbs	
Salt and pepper	Hot water crust
1 small onion	pastry (*see* Raised Game Pie)

Cut the meat into neat small dice and season to taste with herbs, salt and pepper. Place the bones, finely chopped onion, salt and pepper in a saucepan with the water or stock and simmer for 2 hr, so that the gravy when cold will form a firm jelly. Mould the pastry with the hands or line a pie mould. Put in the filling, add some stock and cover with pastry lid. (The remainder of the stock should be reheated and added after the pie is baked and still hot.) 3 or 4 folds of greased greaseproof paper should be fastened round the pie to preserve its shape and prevent it becoming too brown. Brush the top of the pie with egg, or milk, and make a hole in the centre. Bake in a hot oven (220 °C, 425 °F, Gas 7) at first and reduce heat as soon as

pastry is set to moderate (180 °C, 350 °F, Gas 4) for about 1½ hr. Remove the grease-proof paper or mould for the last ½ hr and brush the sides with egg or milk.

If preferred, small individual pies may be made. Cook for about 1 hr.

6 helpings

VEAL AND HAM PIE

2½ lb neck *or* breast of veal	Grated rind of 1 lemon
Salt and pepper	
1½ lb ham *or* bacon	
2 hard-boiled eggs	
Forcemeat balls	
Puff pastry	
Pinch of ground mace	

Cut the meat into 1½-in square pieces. Put into a fireproof dish or saucepan, season with salt and pepper, cover with cold water, and cook gently either in the oven or on the stove for 2 hr. Meanwhile cut the ham into narrow strips, the eggs into thin slices, make the forcemeat balls, and fry them lightly in a little hot dripping. Roll out the pastry to a suitable thickness and cut a piece to cover the top of the pie-dish. Line the edge of the dish with the trimmings. Allow the meat to cool slightly, then cover the bottom of the pie-dish with meat, add a few strips of bacon and slices of egg. Sprinkle lightly with salt, pepper, mace, lemon rind, then intersperse with forcemeat balls. Repeat until the dish is full then half-fill the dish with gravy. Put on a pastry cover, moisten and press the edges together. Make a hole in the centre of the top, decorate with pastry leaves, brush over with egg, and bake for 45–60 min in a fairly hot oven (190 °C, 375 °F, Gas 5). As soon as the pie is baked add a little more well-seasoned gravy through the hole in the top, and when served hot serve with gravy made from the liquor in which the meat was stewed.

A Veal and Ham Pie can also be made in the same way as Pork Pie, for serving cold, using the same quantity of meat in all.

8–10 helpings

Poultry and Game Dishes

ROAST CHICKEN

1 roasting chicken	½ pt chicken stock
Salt and pepper	Fat for basting
2–3 rashers of	
bacon	

Garnish

Bunches of	Bread sauce
washed	
watercress	
Gravy	

Truss chicken for roasting, season lightly and cover with bacon. Roast on a trivet in the roasting tin, in a fairly hot oven (190–200 °C, 375–400 °F, Gas 5–6) for 1–1½ hr until tender. Baste frequently. The chicken may be roasted on the breast for a short while at the beginning. This will make the breast meat more moist. (Prick the thigh to test for tenderness; if there is any trace of blood the chicken is not cooked.) The bacon may be removed 10–15 min before serving, to allow the breast to brown. When the chicken is cooked, place on a hot meat dish, remove the trussing string, and keep the bird hot. Make the gravy: pour excess fat from roasting tin but retain sediment; pour in stock, boil 2–3 min. Season to taste, and strain into a hot sauce-boat.

Have ready the watercress washed, drained and lightly seasoned. Garnish the chicken. Serve with the gravy and bread sauce, and with potato crisps, baked tomatoes, grilled mushrooms and bacon rolls if you wish.

To roast a chicken quickly, joint it and season the pieces. Lay them in a roasting tin with 2 rashers of streaky bacon cut into dice. Bake at 190 °C, 375 °F, Gas 5, for about 40 min, basting when necessary with chicken fat or butter. Cover with a buttered paper, if the chicken looks dry. When cooked, make the gravy as above.

5–6 helpings

ROAST DUCK WITH APPLE SAUCE OR ORANGE GARNISH

1 duck	Salt and pepper
Sage and onion	Apple sauce *or*
stuffing	orange garnish
½ oz flour	(*see* **below**)
½ pt stock	

Fill duck with sage and onion stuffing, truss for roasting. Baste well with hot fat, roast in a fairly hot oven (190–200 °C, 375–400 °F, Gas 5–6) for 1–1½ hr, basting frequently. Keep the duck hot, pour fat from roasting tin, sprinkle in flour and brown it. Stir in stock, simmer 3–4 min, season and strain. Remove trussing strings from duck. Serve gravy and apple sauce separately.

Orange garnish

For the orange garnish for roast duck, use 1 large orange and 1 tablesp brandy or red wine. Remove the yellow skin (only) from the orange with an apple or potato peeler. Stand the orange in boiling water for 1½ min, then wipe dry and remove all white pith. Divide into segments. Cut the skin into thin strips and let them stand in the boiling water for 5 min while the orange segments soak in the brandy or wine.

When you remove the trussing strings from the duck, warm the orange slightly in the brandy, add the strips of peel, and pile both in a shallow, warmed dish as a garnish for the duck.

4–5 helpings   **Cooking time 1½ hr**

ROAST GOOSE

1 goose	Flour
Sage and onion stuffing	Apple sauce
Fat for basting	Gravy (see below)

Prepare the goose, make the stuffing and insert this in the body of the bird. Truss the goose, and prick the skin of the breast. Roast the bird in a fairly hot oven (190–200 °C, 375–400 °F, Gas 5–6) for 2½ hr or until tender. When almost cooked, dredge the breast with flour, baste with some of the hot fat and finish cooking. Remove trussing string; dish the bird. Serve with apple sauce and a gravy made with thickened beef stock. Goose giblet gravy is very rich.

8–10 helpings

ROAST TURKEY WITH CHESTNUTS

1 turkey	2 oz butter
2–3 lb chestnuts, dried or fresh	1 egg
½ pt chicken stock	Salt and pepper
	Cream or milk

1–1½ lb sausage meat or 1 lb veal forcemeat	2–3 slices bacon
	Fat for basting
	Gravy

If fresh, slit the chestnut skins, cook them in boiling water for 15 min, drain and remove the skins. If dried, soak overnight, then simmer for 15 min in fresh water.

Stew the prepared chestnuts in stock for 1 hr; drain, and then chop or sieve them, keeping a few back for garnish. Make the stuffing with the chopped chestnuts, butter (melted), egg, seasoning and cream. Fill the crop of the bird with this stuffing and the body with sausage meat or forcemeat, well seasoned. Truss the bird for roasting. Cover it with bacon, and roast in a moderate oven (180 °C, 350 °F, Gas 4) until tender (15 min per lb under 14 lb, 12 min over 14 lb). Towards the end of the cooking time, remove the bacon to let the breast brown. Remove the trussing string before dishing the bird. Garnish with the reserved chestnuts, and serve with gravy.

CHICKEN À LA MINUTE

3 baby chickens (poussins)	½ pt milk (approx)
2 oz butter	4 button onions
1 oz flour	2 egg yolks
Salt and pepper	¼ pt cream

Cut the prepared chickens into quarters. Melt the butter in a fireproof casserole, fry chicken in butter until golden brown. Sprinkle with flour, salt and pepper and stir until flour is golden brown. Just cover with boiling milk, add the blanched onions, cover tightly and cook gently until tender (20 min–½ hr). Remove onions, remove chicken and keep hot. Stir egg yolks and cream together; add to pan; heat gently until thick. Return chicken and leave over heat without boiling for a few more minutes. Season and serve.

6 helpings   **Cooking time about ¾ hr**

above: Roast chicken, dressed in splendour for formal serving

below: A boiled fowl, luxurious with oysters

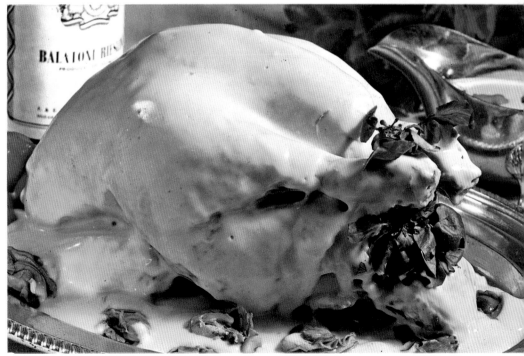

ROAST GUINEA FOWL

1 guinea fowl	Salt and pepper
2 oz butter	2 slices fat bacon

Garnish

Fresh tarragon	Bread sauce
French dressing	Espagnole sauce
Browned	
breadcrumbs	

Prepare the bird, mix the butter and seasoning, and place it in the body of the bird. Truss the bird, lay slices of bacon over the breast, and roast in a moderately hot oven (180–190° C, 350–375 °F, Gas 4–5) for 1–1½ hr, basting frequently. When the bird is almost cooked, 'froth' the breast (i.e. dredge with flour), baste and finish cooking. Wash and dry the tarragon, toss lightly in French dressing. Remove trussing strings from bird and garnish. Serve with it, browned crumbs bread sauce, and Espagnole sauce.

GRILLED CHICKEN WITH MUSHROOM SAUCE

1 frying chicken	Croûte of fried
½ pt Espagnole	bread
sauce	½ lb lean raw ham
One 7–8 oz can	Salad oil or butter
grilling	for frying and
mushrooms	grilling
Salt and pepper	

Garnish

Ham	Watercress

Make Espagnole sauce, add the canned mushrooms to it, correct seasoning, and keep the sauce hot. Divide the chicken into pieces convenient for serving, brush them with salad oil or clarified butter. Cut a slice of bread to fit the serving-dish. Fry this until lightly browned. Cut the ham into short strips and fry it lightly. Grill the prepared chicken until tender (15–20 min). Pile the chicken pieces on the croûte, strain the sauce round, and garnish with the ham and with watercress.

4 helpings

Cooking time about 30 min

DEVILLED TURKEY LEGS

2 turkey legs	Mixed mustard or
Salt and pepper	French mustard
Cayenne pepper	Butter

Remove skin from turkey, criss-cross with deep cuts. Sprinkle well with seasoning and a little cayenne pepper, if you like dishes very hot. Spread with mixed mustard (or French mustard) pressing well into the cuts and leave for several hours. Grill 8–12 min until crisp and brown, spread with small pieces of butter mixed with cayenne, and serve immediately.

4 helpings

CHICKEN 'EN CASSEROLE'

1 chicken	4–6 shallots or
1 oz flour	small onions
Salt and pepper	2 oz chopped
2 oz butter or	mushrooms
dripping	1 pt stock
4–6 oz bacon	

Joint the chicken, and dip the joints in flour and seasoning. Melt the fat in a casserole; fry the bacon, cut in strips; add chicken, mushrooms and chopped shallots or onions. Fry until golden brown, turning when necessary. Add hot stock, sufficient just to cover the chicken, simmer until tender—about 1½ hr. Correct the seasoning. Serve in casserole.

6 helpings

CHICKEN MARENGO

1 chicken	½ glass sherry
¼ pt olive oil	(optional)
1 pt Espagnole	1 doz button
sauce	mushrooms
Salt and pepper	6 stoned olives
2 ripe tomatoes	

Garnish

Fleurons of pastry	Olives
or croûtes of fried	Mushrooms
bread	

Joint the chicken. Remove skin and excess fat. Fry joints in oil until golden brown, drain well, pour away oil. Heat the Espagnole sauce with the tomato pulp, add chicken, sherry (if used), whole olives and mushrooms, and season. Simmer gently until the chicken is tender—about $\frac{3}{4}$ hr. Pile in the centre of a hot dish, strain sauce over and garnish. Place fleurons or croûtes round the dish.

6 helpings

BRAISED TURKEY OR CHICKEN

1 small frozen turkey *or* chicken	Bouquet garni
2–4 oz butter	Salt and pepper
2 onions, sliced	Stock *or* cider and
2 carrots, sliced	stock
1 turnip, sliced	2 slices streaky
	bacon

Truss the thawed bird as for roasting. Melt the butter in a large pan or roasting tin, and brown the bird in the fat. Remove it, place vegetables, bouquet garni and seasoning in pan, adding sufficient stock to almost cover the vegetables. Lay bacon slices on the bird's breast, lay it on the vegetables, cover and cook gently on top of the stove or in a moderate oven (180 °C, 350 °F, Gas 4) until it is tender. Remove the trussing string, and dish the bird.

8 helpings

CHICKEN PILAFF

1 chicken *or* fowl	6 black pepper-
3 pt stock *or* 3 pt water and 2 lb scrag end neck of mutton	corns
	4 oz butter
	6 oz long grain rice
2 large mild onions	Salt and pepper
1 carrot	1 tablesp curry paste
Pinch of ground mace	2 small onions (shallots)

Joint the chicken. Put the backbone, giblets, bones and trimmings and stock (or water and the mutton cut into small pieces) into a saucepan; add outside layers of Spanish onions, carrot, mace and peppercorns. Simmer gently 2–3 hr, strain. Dice the remainder of the onions, fry in a saucepan until lightly browned in 2 oz of the butter, add the washed

and drained rice, $1\frac{1}{2}$ pt stock and seasoning. Cook gently until rice has absorbed stock. Fry chicken slowly in remaining butter until lightly brown. Mix well with curry paste and a little stock, retaining the butter. Cook gently until chicken joints are tender, adding more stock if necessary. Add the rice 10 min before the chicken is done. Cut small onions into rings, fry until golden brown in the butter in which the chicken was fried. Pile the pilaff on a hot dish, pile rings of fried onion on top. Serve very hot.

6 helpings   Cooking time about $1\frac{1}{2}$ hr, excluding stock

CURRIED CHICKEN OR TURKEY

1 chicken *or* 3 lb turkey meat	1 tablesp lemon juice
2 oz butter	Salt and pepper
1 chopped onion	1 oz sultanas
1 dessertsp flour	1 oz blanched
1 tablesp curry powder	almonds
	1 dessertsp
1 dessertsp curry paste	desiccated coconut
$\frac{3}{4}$ pt white stock	2 tablesp cream
1 chopped apple	*or* milk (optional)
1 dessertsp chutney	

Garnish

Fans of lemon	Red pepper
Gherkin fans	

Divide the chicken into neat joints, remove skin, fry joints lightly in hot butter, remove from saucepan and drain. Fry the onion lightly, add flour, curry powder and paste, and fry very well, stirring occasionally. Stir in the stock, bring to the boil. Put in all other ingredients except the cream. (Have the coconut tied in muslin, and remove after 15 min.) Put in chicken. Simmer gently about $1\frac{1}{4}$ hr, adding a little more stock if necessary. Dish the chicken, add the cream to the sauce and pour the sauce over the chicken, after straining if liked.

Accompaniments

Dry boiled rice sprinkled with paprika and pepper, mango chutney, Bombay Duck,

Chicken 'en casserole'

Pappadums, fresh grated coconut, gherkins, pickled pimentoes. These are served separately, not in the dish with the curry. Bombay Duck and Pappadums are fried before serving.

6 helpings   **Cooking time** $1\frac{3}{4}$ **hr**

BRAISED DUCK WITH CHESTNUTS AND FRUIT

1 duck	1 glass port wine
1 pt stock	(optional)
Larding bacon	1 dessertsp
(optional)	redcurrant jelly
2 oz butter	
$\frac{3}{4}$ pt Espagnole	
sauce	

Mirepoix

2 onions	Bouquet garni
1 small turnip	6 black
2 carrots	peppercorns
1 stick celery	2 cloves

Stuffing

1 lb chestnuts	Salt and pepper
1 large mild onion	1 egg

Garnish

Watercress	Grapes, apple *or*
Forcemeat balls	orange slices

Boil the chestnuts, remove the skins and chop or mince all but 6 nuts finely for stuffing. Cook the onion in water until tender, chop finely, add to chestnuts, season well and bind with egg. Stuff duck with chestnut mixture, truss, lard with bacon, if liked. Slice the vegetables for the mirepoix foundation, place in a large saucepan with butter, lay the duck on the vegetables, cover the pan; fry gently for 20 min; then add bouquet garni, spices, and enough stock to cover $\frac{3}{4}$ of the depth of the mirepoix. Cover with a buttered paper, put on lid, simmer gently until duck is tender, for about 2 hr. Add more stock if necessary to prevent burning. Heat the Espagnole sauce, add the 6 nuts, wine (if used) and jelly, re-heat and season to taste. When duck is ready, remove paper and trussing string, and place it in a hot oven (220–230 °C, 425–450 °F, Gas 7–8) to crisp the bacon. Serve on a hot dish, with a watercress or fruit garnish, and forcemeat balls. Serve sauce separately.

4–5 helpings

BOILED FOWL WITH OYSTERS

1 fowl	$\frac{3}{4}$ pt Béchamel
2 doz canned	sauce
oysters	$\frac{1}{8}$ pt cream *or*
Pinch of ground	milk
mace	1 egg
1 oz butter	Salt and pepper

Place about 1 dozen oysters inside the bird and truss it for boiling. Put the bird with mace and butter into a deep earthenware casserole with a close-fitting lid. Place this in a baking tin of boiling water, cook on the stove or in a moderate oven (180 °C, 350 °F, Gas 4) until the fowl is tender (about $2\frac{1}{2}$ hr). Remove trussing string from cooked fowl, dish and keep it hot. Strain the liquor from the fowl, stir it into the Béchamel sauce, heat thoroughly and stir in cream or milk blended with the egg. Continue stirring and heating, until the sauce thickens; do not allow it to boil, or it may curdle. Season. Pour some sauce over the fowl, add the oysters and their liquor to the remainder, and serve separately.

5–6 helpings

CHICKEN WITH SUPRÊME SAUCE

1 chicken	**$1\frac{1}{2}$ pt white stock**
$\frac{3}{4}$ pt Suprême	**(approx)**
sauce	

Garnish

Macédoine of vegetables *or* **grape garnish as below**

Truss the chicken, poach it in the stock until tender, then divide into neat joints. Arrange the joints on a hot dish, pour the sauce over, and garnish with the chopped macédoine of vegetable piled at either end of the dish.

As an alternative garnish, toss 1 chopped red pepper and 1 cooked potato (sliced) in the sauce before pouring it over the chicken. Top with black and green grapes.

4–6 helpings
Cooking time about $1\frac{1}{2}$–2 hr

POULTRY HOT-POT

1 boiling fowl	**$\frac{1}{2}$ pt stock** *or* **water**
3 rashers of bacon	**$\frac{1}{2}$ oz butter**
Salt and pepper	**$\frac{1}{2}$ oz flour**
Nutmeg	**2 teasp chopped**
2 shallots	**parsley**

Place the giblets from the fowl in the bottom of a casserole. Joint the fowl, remove skin and put joints into casserole, adding bacon (cut in strips), salt, pepper, nutmeg, sliced shallots and the hot stock (or water). Cover tightly, cook in a fairly hot oven (190–200 °C, 375–400 °F, Gas 5–6) for about 2 hr. Knead together butter and flour and add in small pieces to the hot-pot. Add parsley and cook for another $\frac{1}{2}$ hr. Correct seasoning and serve.

Chicken Marengo in the making

This may be served with plain boiled long grain rice.

6 helpings

FRICASSÉE OF COOKED CHICKEN

1 boiled *or* **one**	**$\frac{1}{2}$ gill cream** *or*
1 lb can of	**milk**
chicken	**1 egg**
1 pt Velouté	**Salt and pepper**
sauce	**Juice of 1 lemon**

Garnish

Chopped parsley
Sippets of fried
bread *or*
creamed potato
border

Cut the chicken into joints, remove skin and excess fat. Make sauce, thoroughly heat

73

chicken in it, add cream and egg, stir over a low heat until the sauce thickens but do not boil. Season, add lemon juice. Arrange chicken in an entrée dish, strain sauce over and garnish.

If a potato border is used, pipe or fork this into the dish, before arranging the chicken for serving.

6 helpings
Cooking time 20 min (excluding sauce)

CHICKEN PIE

1 large or 2 small chickens	Puff pastry using 8 oz flour, etc.
Veal forcemeat	Salt and pepper
$\frac{1}{2}$ lb ham or bacon	$\frac{3}{4}$ pt chicken
2 hard-boiled eggs	stock
	Egg for glazing

Joint the chicken; boil bones, gizzards, and trimmings for stock. Parboil the chicken liver, chop finely and mix with veal forcemeat. Cut ham into strips and eggs into sections. Make pastry. Arrange chicken and other ingredients in layers in a 1 pt pie-dish, seasoning each layer carefully, then three-quarters fill the dish with stock. Cover pie-dish with pastry, slit the top, decorate and glaze with beaten egg yolk. Bake $1\frac{1}{2}$–2 hr until meat is cooked. Until the pastry is set, have the oven hot (220 °C, 425 °F, Gas 7), then lower the heat (180–190 °C, 350–375 °F, Gas 4–5) until cooking is complete. Before serving, add remainder of hot stock to pie.

6–8 helpings Cooking time about $2\frac{1}{2}$ hr

CHICKEN VOL-AU-VENT

6 oz cooked chicken	2–4 oz mushrooms
Puff pastry, frozen or using 8 oz flour, etc	Salt, pepper, nutmeg
2 oz cooked ham or tongue	$\frac{1}{2}$ pt Béchamel sauce
1 oz cooked noodles	Egg or milk to glaze

Prepare the pastry; roll out to $\frac{3}{4}$ in thickness. Cut into a round or oval shape and place on a wet baking sheet. Cut an inner ring through

half the depth of the pastry and brush top of pastry (not sides) with beaten egg. Bake in a hot oven (220–230 °C, 425–450 °F, Gas 7) until well risen, firm and brown (about 25 min). Dice chicken and ham, slice mushrooms; add all these with the noodles to the Béchamel sauce, season well and heat thoroughly. Lift centre from vol-au-vent case and reserve for lid, clear any soft paste which may be inside, fill with the mixture, and replace lid.

A separate piece of pastry the size of the lid may be baked with the large case, and used as a lid for the filled case; this has a better appearance.

Alternatively make the pastry into six individual cases, and use the following filling:

Filling

One $10\frac{1}{2}$ oz can condensed Cream of Mushroom soup	2 oz cooked ham, diced
	1–2 tablesp cream (optional)
8 oz cooked chicken or turkey meat, diced	

Heat the chicken and ham gently in the soup, then add the cream if used. Fill the prepared cases. Put them into a preheated moderate oven (180 °C, 350 °F, Gas 4) to warm through and crisp. Serve hot or cold, with a crisp salad.

6 helpings

CHICKEN SALAD

$\frac{3}{4}$ lb cold cooked chicken	1 tablesp vinegar
	Seasoning
3 tablesp chopped celery	6 tablesp mayonnaise
1 hard-boiled egg	
1 tablesp salad oil	

Garnish—selection of

Gherkins	Stoned olives
Capers	Lettuce
Anchovy fillets	

Cut chicken into neat pieces; mix with celery, the chopped egg white, salad oil, vinegar and seasoning. Allow to stand for

1 hr. Stir in the mayonnaise. Pile the mixture on a bed of lettuce, garnish with a selection of the ingredients suggested, and sprinkle the sieved egg yolk over. Chill before serving.

4 helpings

DUCK SALAD

2 slices bread, $\frac{1}{4}$ in thick	1 in cucumber cut in strips
Oil for frying	1 oz walnuts, chopped
6-8 oz cooked duck *or* goose	4 tablesp whipped salad dressing (commercial)
3-4 tomatoes, skinned and quartered	Lettuce leaves
4-5 spring onions	

Remove crusts from the bread, and cut into $\frac{1}{4}$-in dice. Heat the oil in a frying-pan, and fry the bread cubes until golden brown on all sides. Cut up the duck, into biggish pieces or slices. Cool the fried bread cubes, and toss with the duck in the salad dressing. Line a bowl with crisp, washed lettuce leaves, and place the salad in the centre.

ROAST GROUSE OR PARTRIDGE

1 grouse *or* partridge
1 rasher of bacon
Butter *or* dripping
Toasted *or* fried
bread croûte
Trimmings as
below

Pluck, draw and truss the bird as for roasting a chicken. Cover its breast with bacon; roast in a fairly hot oven (190-200 °C, 375-400 °F, Gas 5-6) for about 30 min, basting frequently with butter or dripping. (A piece of seasoned butter may be put in the body of the bird if liked.) About 10 min before serving, remove bacon, baste, dredge with flour, baste and return to oven to complete cooking. Remove trussing string. Dish the bird on the croûte. Serve with brown gravy, bread sauce and fried breadcrumbs.

1 or 2 helpings

ROAST PHEASANT

1 pheasant	1 slice bacon *or*
$\frac{1}{4}$ lb beef steak	strips of larding
or 12 mushrooms,	bacon
chopped and	French dressing
seasoned	Trimmings as
(optional) and	below
2 oz butter	
Butter *or* dripping	

Garnish

Watercress

Pluck and draw the bird, but leave the head on. Insert the steak in the body of the bird to improve the flavour and keep the bird moist, or stuff with mushrooms and butter. The steak can be used for a cold meat dish later. Truss the pheasant as for a roasting chicken. Cover the breast with strips of bacon, or lard it with the prepared larding bacon. Roast the bird in a moderate oven (180 °C, 350 °F, Gas 4) until tender (40-50 min), basting when necessary. When bird is almost cooked, 'froth' the breast. Remove trussing string.

Garnish with watercress tossed in French dressing, and serve with brown gravy, bread sauce and fried breadcrumbs. If preferred, the head may be removed and the bird ornamented with the best tail feathers before serving. The feathers should be washed, baked until dry in a cool oven, and stuck fanwise into the vent end of the cooked bird.

4-5 helpings   Cooking time 40-50 min

ROAST WILD DUCK

2 wild duck	Trimmings as
Croûtes of fried	below
bread	
Butter for	
basting	

Pluck and draw the birds, cut off the heads. Cut off the toes, scald and scrape the feet, truss the birds with the feet twisted underneath the body. If the fishy taste is disliked, cover a deep roasting tin to a depth of $\frac{1}{2}$ in with boiling water, add 1 tablesp salt, put

75

above: Roast wild duck   below: Chicken pie   Chicken with suprême sauce

in the birds and bake them for 10 min, basting frequently with the salt water. Drain, sprinkle lightly with flour, baste well with hot butter and roast in a moderate oven (180 °C, 350 °F, Gas 4) for 20–30 min, basting frequently. The birds should always be served rather underdone, or the flavour is lost. The breast meat has much the best flavour. Serve on croûtes with a well-flavoured rich sauce, bacon rolls, fried croûtes cut in triangles, and Orange Salad.

COMPOTE OF PIGEONS OR PARTRIDGES

3 pigeons	Bouquet garni
or partridges	1 carrot
$\frac{1}{4}$ lb raw ham *or*	$\frac{1}{2}$ turnip
bacon	Croûtes of fried
12 shallots *or*	bread
small onions	
$1\frac{1}{2}$ oz butter	
1 pt good stock	
1 oz flour	
Salt and pepper	

Truss birds for roasting, dice ham or bacon and peel shallots or onions. Melt butter, fry birds, bacon and onions until well-browned. Add stock, bring to boiling point; add the bouquet garni, diced carrot and turnip. Cover and allow to simmer steadily until birds are tender, for $\frac{3}{4}$–1 hr. Remove birds and onions; cut away trussing strings and split birds in half. Keep hot. Blend flour with a little cold water or stock, add to pan. Bring to boiling point, stirring continuously, re-cover and allow to simmer for 10 min. Season to taste, skim off any excess fat. Serve on a hot dish, pour the sauce over, garnish with the onions and with croûtes of fried bread.

6 helpings

JUGGED PIGEONS

3 pigeons	Salt and pepper
3 oz butter	1 oz flour
1 onion	1 glass port *or*
1 carrot	claret (optional)
1 pt good beef	
stock	

Garnish

Balls of fried veal forcemeat (optional)

Truss the pigeons as for roasting and fry them until well-browned in 2 oz of the butter. Place the birds in a casserole. Brown the sliced onion and carrot in butter, and add to the pigeons, together with stock and seasoning. Cover and cook in a moderate oven (180 °C, 350 °F, Gas 4) for $1\frac{3}{4}$ hr. Knead together the flour and remaining 1 oz butter and drop in small pieces into the stock; continue cooking $\frac{1}{2}$ hr, adding wine if used, half-way through this period. Serve pigeons with the sauce poured over, garnished with forcemeat balls if you wish.

6 helpings

SALMI OF PHEASANT

1 pheasant	$\frac{1}{2}$ pt brown sauce
2 oz butter	1 glass Madeira
$\frac{1}{4}$ teasp grated	(optional)
lemon rind	6–8 slices goose
2 shallots	liver *or* pâté
$\frac{1}{4}$ teasp thyme	6–8 mushrooms
1 bay leaf	Salt and pepper

Garnish

Croûtes of fried bread (triangular) *or* fleurons of pastry

Pluck, draw and truss bird for roasting. Baste it well with hot butter; roast in a hot oven (220–230 °C, 425–450 °F, Gas 7–8) for 30 min, basting frequently. Pour the butter used for basting into a saucepan, add grated lemon rind, chopped shallots, thyme and bay leaf. Joint the bird, lay aside breast, wings and legs, and cut remainder into neat pieces; add these to the saucepan and fry. If any fat remains, pour it from the saucepan, put in the brown sauce, wine (if used), and season. Simmer for 10 min. Add remainder of pheasant, heat thoroughly. Meanwhile, reheat the butter, fry in it the slices of goose liver if used, and the mushrooms. Correct seasoning of sauce. Serve pheasant with pâté or liver; strain the sauce over, garnish with the croûtes or fleurons and the mushrooms.

4–5 helpings
Cooking time about $1\frac{1}{4}$ hr in all

PIGEON PIE

2 pigeons	Puff pastry,
$\frac{1}{2}$ lb rump steak	frozen *or* using
$\frac{1}{4}$ lb ham *or* bacon	8 oz flour, etc
$\frac{3}{4}$ pt good stock	Egg *or* milk to
Salt and pepper	glaze
2 hard-boiled	
eggs	

Remove the feet from the pigeons and split each bird in two. Cut the steak in small thin slices, cut the bacon in strips and slice the eggs. Put all the ingredients in a pie-dish in layers; season the layers well, and season each half-bird; $\frac{3}{4}$ fill the dish with stock. Cover pie with puff pastry, slit, glaze, and cook in a hot oven (220–230 °C, 425–450 °F, Gas 7–8) until the pastry is risen and set; then lower heat to moderate (180–190 °C, 350–375 °F, Gas 4–5) and bake for 1 hr more under buttered paper. Fill up with hot stock.

For an old-style display, cut the toes off the feet, and scald the latter. Before serving the pie, fix the feet in an upright position in the hole previously made in the pastry for pouring in stock.

6 helpings

RAISED GAME PIE

1 lb well-hung	2 hard-boiled
game birds	eggs
(pheasant	1 dessertsp
or partridge)	mixed herbs
$\frac{3}{4}$ lb chicken livers	6 thin rashers
1 small onion	streaky bacon
1 clove garlic	$\frac{1}{4}$ oz gelatine
$\frac{1}{2}$ lb sausage	$\frac{1}{2}$ oz flour
meat	

Hot Water Crust Pastry

10 oz plain flour	$\frac{1}{4}$ pt milk and
1 level teasp salt	water
Pinch of black	3 oz lard
pepper	Egg for glazing
1 egg yolk	

Cut meat from birds, discarding gristle and skin. Shred finely. Mince or chop the livers, onion and garlic with a little flour to prevent sticking. Mix livers, sausage meat, chopped eggs and herbs.

Warm the flour, and sift with the salt and pepper. Mix the egg yolk with 1 tablesp liquid, and boil the remaining milk and water with the lard. When the lard is melted, pour the mixture into the dry ingredients, and mix well with a wooden spoon. Add the egg mixture and knead quickly until smooth. Keep warm in a basin covered with a folded tea towel over a basin of hot water for $\frac{1}{2}$ hr. To use, roll out $\frac{3}{4}$ of the pastry and line a raised pie mould or 7-in diameter cake-tin with a slip-out bottom. Line the bottom and sides of the pastry with bacon, and put in a layer of the liver mixture. Then put in a layer of the game. Repeat the layers, finishing with a game one. Do not fill the pie to the top. Roll out the remaining $\frac{1}{4}$ of the pastry. Brush edges with beaten egg, and cover the pie. Trim the edges, and brush with beaten egg. Cut leaves from the trimmings, and decorate the pie with them. Brush again with beaten egg, and make a hole in the centre of the lid for steam to escape.

Bake for 1 hr at 190 °C, 375 °F, Gas 5; reduce heat to 180 °C, 350 °F, Gas 4 for a further 1–1$\frac{1}{4}$ hr. While the pie is baking, boil the carcases of the game and simmer until $\frac{1}{2}$ pt liquid remains. Strain. Soften the gelatine in 2 tablesp cold water, stir into the stock and stir until dissolved.

If the pie is to be eaten hot, stir a little hot stock in the $\frac{1}{2}$ oz flour, and cook over gentle heat for 1 min. Add enough hot stock to make a thick sauce, and pour this into the hot pie through the hole in the lid.

If the pie is required cold, leave it to cool, and pour in the cooled stock when it is just on the point of setting. Leave in a cool place for about 12 hr.

6–8 helpings   Cooking time 2–2$\frac{1}{4}$ hr

ROAST HAUNCH OF VENISON

A haunch of	Flour
venison	Brown sauce *or*
Clarified butter	gravy
or dripping	Redcurrant jelly

Saw off the knuckle-bone, brush joint well

with clarified butter or dripping and wrap in well-greased paper. Make a stiff paste of flour and water, put it over the joint, cover with another well-greased paper and tie securely with string. Roast the joint in a moderate oven (180 °C, 350 °F, Gas 4) for 3–4 hr depending on size and baste frequently. After 2½ hr remove paste and papers, dredge lightly with flour, baste well with hot butter, and roast until the joint is a rich brown colour. Serve as hot as possible. Serve gravy or brown sauce and redcurrant jelly separately.

12 (or more) helpings
Cooking time 25 min per lb

STEWED VENISON

Shoulder of venison	Salt and pepper
	1½ pt game stock
Thin slices of	½ teasp
mutton fat	peppercorns
1 glass port	½ teasp allspice
(optional)	Redcurrant jelly

If port is used, soak the mutton fat in it for 2–3 hr. Bone the venison, flatten with a cutlet-bat, season well, cover with slices of mutton fat. Roll up lightly, tie securely with tape, place in boiling stock together with bones, peppercorns, allspice and the port in which the fat was soaked. Simmer gently for 3–3½ hr. Serve with redcurrant jelly, handed separately.

10–12 helpings

JUGGED HARE

1 hare	12 peppercorns
3 oz butter	Bouquet garni
Salt and pepper	1½ pt stock
1 onion	1 oz flour
4 cloves	Veal forcemeat
1 glass port *or*	Fat for frying
claret (optional)	Redcurrant jelly
1 tablesp lemon juice	

top left: Raised game pie
top right: Jugged pigeons
bottom left: Salmi of pheasant with croûtes
bottom right: Compote of pigeons

Prepare the hare and cut into neat small pieces. Heat 2 oz of the butter, and fry the pieces of hare in it until brown. Put the hare in a casserole with salt, onion stuck with cloves, half the wine (if used), lemon juice, peppercorns, bouquet garni and hot stock. Place a tight lid on the casserole, cook in a moderate oven (180 °C, 350 °F, Gas 4) about 3 hr. Knead the flour and remaining butter together, stir into the stock about $\frac{1}{2}$ hr before serving. Add the remaining wine too, and season to taste. Form forcemeat into small balls and fry. Gently heat the blood from hare, stir into the gravy, allow to thicken. Serve hare piled on a hot dish, strain sauce over, and arrange the forcemeat balls round dish. Serve with redcurrant jelly handed separately.

5–6 helpings

FRICASSÉE OF RABBIT

$\frac{1}{2}$ **lb celery**	**1 blade mace** or
1 tablesp cooking	**pinch ground**
oil	**mace**
1 small onion,	**Salt and pepper**
chopped	**1 lb cooked**
2 oz margarine	**rabbit without**
2 oz flour	**bone**
2 oz skim milk	$\frac{1}{4}$ **lb streaky bacon**
powder with	**Triangles of toast**
water to make	
1 pt liquid	

Wash and chop the celery. Heat the oil in a saucepan, add the onion and celery and cook slowly without browning. Lift out the vegetables, and reserve. Add the margarine to the pan, stir in the flour, and cook for 2 min. Remove from heat, add the liquid skim milk, then bring to the boil slowly, stirring continuously. Simmer for 3 min, add mace and season to taste. Stir in the cooked vegetables.

Cut the rabbit into bite-sized pieces, and stir into the sauce. Keep warm. Remove the rind from the bacon, flatten with a knife, cut into 3-in lengths and roll up for threading on a skewer. Cook under a hot grill until crisp, turning once or twice. Put the rabbit and sauce in the centre of a large dish. Arrange toast triangles round the edge and place bacon rolls on top. Serve immediately.

If desired, the rabbit can be prepared ahead of time, and reheated when the bacon is grilled.

3–4 helpings

RABBIT STEW—RICH

1 rabbit	**1 pt good stock**
4 oz streaky	**Bouquet garni**
bacon	**2 cloves**
18 button onions	**Salt and pepper**
2 oz butter	**1 glass claret**
$1\frac{1}{2}$ **oz flour**	**(optional)**

Wash, dry and joint the rabbit, put the liver aside. Dice the bacon, peel the onions. Melt the butter in a large saucepan, fry onions and bacon until brown, then lift out. Fry rabbit lightly, sprinkle in flour and continue frying until well browned. Replace the onions and bacon, add hot stock, bouquet garni, cloves and seasoning, cover tightly and stew gently until rabbit is tender (about $1\frac{1}{4}$ hr). About 15 min before serving, add the claret if used, put in the liver (washed and cut into small pieces) and finish cooking. Pile the rabbit on a hot dish, strain the sauce over and garnish with the bacon dice and onions.

3–4 helpings   Cooking time about 2 hr

RABBIT PIE

1 rabbit	**Egg for glazing**
$\frac{1}{2}$ **lb beef steak**	**Trimmings as**
$\frac{1}{2}$ **lb bacon** or	**below, for cold**
pickled pork	**pie**
Salt and pepper	
$\frac{1}{2}$ **pt stock**	
Puff pastry,	
frozen or **using**	
8 oz flour, etc	

Wash, dry, and joint the rabbit, dice the beef and bacon or pork. Place these ingredients in layers in a pie-dish, season well, $\frac{3}{4}$ fill dish with stock. Cover with pastry; slit and glaze it. Bake $1\frac{1}{4}$–2 hr in a hot oven (220–230 °C, 425–450 °F, Gas 7–8) for 15 min and a moderate oven (180 °C, 350 °F, Gas 4) for the remainer of the time. Add remainder of seasoned stock; serve hot or cold. If the pie is required cold, forcemeat balls and sliced hard-boiled egg will be an improvement.

6–8 helpings   Cooking time $1\frac{3}{4}$–2 hr

Vegetable Dishes

VEGETABLE SIDE DISHES

FRIED ARTICHOKE BOTTOMS IN BATTER

6 artichoke bottoms	Deep fat for frying
Fried parsley	

Batter for coating vegetables

2 oz plain flour	4 tablesp tepid
Pinch of salt and pepper	water (approx)
1 dessertsp olive oil	1 egg white

Cut the cooked artichoke bottoms into 3 or 4 pieces according to size. Sift the flour and seasoning and mix to a smooth batter with the oil and sufficient tepid water to give a coating consistency. Leave to stand for $\frac{1}{2}$ hr. Fold in the stiffly whipped egg white just before frying. Dip the pieces of artichoke into the batter on a skewer and lower each piece carefully into hot deep fat at 180 °C, 340 °F. Turn them during frying as they will float, and when golden-brown (5–7 min) remove from the fat. Drain well and serve garnished with fried parsley.

The bottoms will have more flavour if soaked for $\frac{1}{2}$ hr before coating and frying in a marinade of olive oil, lemon juice, pepper, salt and herbs.

4–6 helpings

BOILED FRENCH OR RUNNER BEANS

1$\frac{1}{2}$ lb French or runner beans	1 oz butter or margarine
	Salt

Wash, top and tail and string the beans. Do not cut up French beans or young runner beans as they lose their flavour in cooking. For older scarlet runners, slice thinly, or, for better flavour, cut into diamonds, i.e. slice them in a slanting direction. Have ready just enough boiling salted water to cover them and cook them with the lid on the pan. When tender (15–20 min), drain and re-heat in butter or margarine. Serve immediately.

For the French method of cooking, drain the cooked beans well, and shake in the pan until most of the water has evaporated. Add a little butter, parsley, lemon juice and seasoning and shake over heat for a few minutes. Serve immediately.

4–6 helpings

83

BROAD BEANS WITH PARSLEY SAUCE

2–3 lb broad beans Salt	2–3 savory leaves (if available) Parsley sauce

Wash the beans and shell them. If not to be cooked immediately, cover over with some of the washed pods as this prevents the skins of the beans from drying out and becoming slightly toughened. Cook gently in just enough boiling salted water to cover, with the savory leaves in the water. When tender, 15–35 min according to size and age, drain well. Make a good parsley sauce with half milk and half bean water and well flavoured with lemon juice. Re-heat the beans in the sauce and serve immediately.

When really young, broad beans should have heads, tails and strings removed as for runner beans, and be cooked whole in the pods. The pods are eaten after tossing them in melted butter. The pod is quite tender, with an excellent flavour, and a very economical dish can be produced by this method. When really mature, it is often necessary to skin the beans after cooking and before tossing them in the parsley sauce.

4–6 helpings (according to yield)

BOILED BRUSSELS SPROUTS WITH CHESTNUTS

1½ lb Brussels sprouts Salt 1 oz butter *or* margarine (optional)	12 cooked chestnuts 3 oz chopped ham 4 tablesp cream

Choose small, close, sprouts. Remove shabby outer leaves by cutting the end, then make a cross-cut on the bottom of each stalk. Soak in cold water, containing 1 teasp of salt per quart, for 10 min only. Wash thoroughly under running water if possible. Choose a suitable-sized pan and put in enough water to ¼ fill it only, with ½ teasp salt to 1 pt of water. When boiling, put in half the sprouts, the largest ones if variable in size, put on lid and bring quickly to boil again. Add rest of

Fried artichoke bottoms in batter

sprouts and cook until all are just tender, with the lid on the pan all the time. Drain in a colander and serve immediately in a hot vegetable dish or toss in melted butter before serving. Sprouts should be served quickly as they soon cool.

To serve with chestnuts put the sprouts, chopped chestnuts, ham and cream into a casserole, cover and re-heat gently in the oven at 180 °C, 350 °F, Gas 4. Do not boil.

6 helpings   Cooking time 15 min

BOILED CABBAGE

1 large, fresh cabbage (about 2 lb)	Salt

Red cabbage with apples

Cut across the end and remove only the very thick, coarse piece of stalk and shrivelled or discoloured outer leaves. Pull off the green leaves and put to soak, with the heart cut into 4 pieces, in cold water with 1 teasp of salt per quart of water. Soak for 10 min only. Choose a suitable sized pan and put in enough water to $\frac{1}{4}$ fill it only, with $\frac{1}{2}$ teasp of salt to 1 pt of water. Cut out the stalk from the green leaves and heart of the cabbage, shred it and put on to cook with the lid on the pan. Shred the green outer leaves and add these to the pan. Replace lid and bring to boil again quickly, while shredding the cabbage heart. Add the heart to the pan a handful at a time so that the water barely goes off the boil. Cook with lid on pan only until the cabbage is just tender. Drain well in a colander but do not press out liquid. Serve in a hot dish and send to table immediately.

6 helpings

RED CABBAGE WITH APPLES

1 small red cabbage	1 tablesp golden syrup
1 oz margarine	Juice of $\frac{1}{2}$ lemon
1 onion chopped very fine	2 tablesp vinegar
2 cooking apples	Salt

Melt the fat. Add the onion and fry gently

until light brown. Add cabbage finely shredded, peeled and sliced apples, and syrup. Cook over very gentle heat for 10 min, shaking pan frequently. Add lemon juice, vinegar and salt and simmer covered, $1-1\frac{1}{2}$ hr. Stir occasionally. Season and serve.

6 helpings

BOILED CAULIFLOWER WITH WHITE SAUCE

1 large cauliflower	Salt
$\frac{1}{2}$ pt white sauce made with half milk and half vegetable water	

Trim off the stem and all the leaves, except the very young ones. Soak in cold water, head down, with 1 teasp salt per qt of water, for not more than 10 min. Wash well. Choose a suitable-sized pan and put in enough water to $\frac{1}{4}$ fill it, with $\frac{1}{2}$ teasp salt to 1 pt water. Put in cauliflower, stalk down, and cook with lid on pan until stalk and flower are tender. Lift out carefully and drain. Keep hot. Coat the cauliflower with the sauce and serve immediately. To reduce cooking time, the cauliflower may be quartered before cooking or broken into large sprigs.

6 helpings

CARROTS—COOKED FOR FOOD VALUE

$1\frac{1}{2}$ lb carrots	1 gill boiling water
1 oz butter or margarine	Chopped parsley
$\frac{1}{2}$ teasp salt	

Cut off the green tops, scrub and scrape the carrots. Slice them thinly if old carrots (or leave whole if really young). Fat steam the carrots for 10 min, i.e. shake them in the melted fat, well below frying temperature, with the lid on the pan until the fat is absorbed. Add the liquid (less for young carrots) and the salt, and simmer gently until the carrots are tender—15-30 min according to age of carrots. Serve hot, with the small amount of liquid remaining, and garnished with parsley.

This method should be employed for cooking most root vegetables. Both flavour and food value are conserved.

6 helpings

BRAISED CELERY

4 heads of celery Stock, meat or vegetable	Meat glaze (if available)

Mirepoix

$\frac{1}{2}$ oz dripping	Bouquet garni
$\frac{1}{2}$ oz bacon	(thyme,
2 large carrots	marjoram,
1 small turnip	sage, parsley)
2 onions	1 bay leaf
A pinch of mace	Watercress to
6 white peppercorns	garnish Salt

Trim the celery but leave the heads whole. Wash them well and tie each securely. Prepare the mirepoix. Fry the bacon in the dripping in a large saucepan, then fry all the vegetables cut in pieces $\frac{3}{4}$ in thick, until lightly browned. Add herbs, spices and $\frac{1}{2}$ teasp of salt and enough stock to come $\frac{3}{4}$ of the way up the vegetables. Bring to boiling point. Lay the celery on top. Baste well with the stock in the pan and cover closely with greased paper or metal foil. Put on lid and cook until the celery is soft (about $1\frac{1}{2}$ hr). Baste several times during cooking. Dish the celery and keep hot. Strain the liquor, put it back in the pan. Reduce by boiling quickly until of glazing consistency or use meat glaze. Pour over the celery. If you wish, place the dish under a hot grill for a moment until it begins to brown. Garnish with watercress.

BOILED LENTILS

$\frac{3}{4}$ lb lentils	1 clove
Bouquet garni	Salt and pepper
1 ham bone (if available) or bacon rinds	$\frac{1}{2}$ oz butter or margarine
1 onion	

Put the lentils into cold water with the herbs, ham bone, onion stuck with the clove, and a little salt. Bring to boiling point and cook until the lentils are soft—about 1 hr. Strain the lentils, toss in a little melted butter *or* margarine; season and serve. If preferred, sieve the lentils before tossing in butter.

6 helpings

VEGETABLE MARROW— COOKED FOR FOOD VALUE

2 small marrows	**$\frac{3}{4}$ pt white sauce**
1 oz butter *or*	**$\frac{1}{2}$–1 gill boiling**
margarine	**water**
$\frac{1}{2}$ teasp salt	

Peel the marrows. Cut into halves lengthwise and scrape out the seeds and pith with a tablespoon. Cut into pieces, about 2 in square. Fat steam the pieces for 10 min, i.e. shake them in the melted fat, well below frying temperature with the lid on the pan until the fat is absorbed. Add the liquid and the salt, and simmer gently until the marrow is tender, about 15 min. Drain well, retaining the cooking liquor for use in making the white sauce. Dish the marrow in a hot dish and coat with the sauce. Serve immediately.

6 helpings

GRILLED MUSHROOMS

12 flat	**Buttered toast**
mushrooms	**Chopped parsley**
Salt and pepper	**Lemon juice**
Butter *or* **bacon**	
fat	

Wash mushrooms, trim the stalks. Season and brush with melted butter *or* bacon fat. Cook under a hot grill, turning them once. Serve in a hot dish or on rounds of buttered toast, with a sprinkling of chopped parsley and a squeeze of lemon juice. A pinch of very finely chopped marjoram, sprinkled on each mushroom prior to grilling, imparts an excellent flavour.

6 helpings

BAKED ONIONS

6 large onions	**A little margarine**
Salt and pepper	*or* **butter**
	A little milk

1 Peel the onions and cook in boiling, salted water for 20 min. Drain and place in a fire-proof dish. Sprinkle with salt and pepper. Put a small pat of margarine *or* butter on the top of each and pour enough milk in the dish to come $\frac{1}{3}$ of the way up the onions. Cover with a greased paper. Bake in a moderate oven (180 °C, 350 °F, Gas 4) until tender (about $1\frac{1}{2}$ hr), basting frequently with the milk. Serve with any milk and onion liquor in the dish.

2 Boil the onions till tender, in their skins. Drain and dry in a cloth and wrap each onion in well-greased paper or in foil. Bake in a moderate oven (180° C, 350° F, Gas 4) for an hour. Unwrap and serve in their skins with butter or margarine.

3 Trim off the roots of the onions, wipe, but do not skin. Put a little margarine, butter *or* dripping in a fireproof dish, or roasting tin. Place the onions in it and bake until tender in a fairly hot oven (180 °C, 355 °F, Gas 5). Take out the onions and peel them. Put them back in the dish, season with salt and pepper, and baste well, using a little extra fat if necessary. Re-heat for 10 min.

6 helpings

GREEN PEAS

2 lb peas	**A little sugar**
Salt	**$\frac{1}{2}$ oz butter** *or*
Sprig of mint	**margarine**

Shell the peas. Have sufficient boiling, salted water to cover the peas. Add the peas, mint and sugar. Simmer gently until soft, from 10–20 min. Drain well. Re-heat with butter *or* margarine and serve in a hot vegetable dish.

If the peas must be shelled some time before cooking, put them in a basin and cover them closely with washed pea-pods.

4–6 helpings (according to yield)

POTATOES BAKED IN THEIR JACKETS

6 large potatoes
Butter *or* **margarine** *or* **bacon fat**

Scrub the potatoes, rinse and dry them. Brush with melted butter, or margarine or bacon fat or rub with a greasy butter paper. Prick with a fork. Bake on the shelves of a fairly hot oven (190 °C, 375 °F, Gas 5) until soft—about $1\frac{1}{2}$ hr. Turn once whilst they are cooking. Make a cut in the top of each, insert a pat of butter or margarine. Serve in a hot vegetable dish.

New potatoes can be cooked in the same way.

6 helpings

BOILED, MASHED OR CREAMED POTATOES

2 lb even-sized potatoes, old *or* **new**	Salt Chopped parsley

Scrub the potatoes. Peel or scrape thinly, if desired. Rinse and put in a saucepan with enough *boiling* water to cover, and 1 teasp salt per qt water. Boil gently for 15–40 min according to age and size. Test with a fine skewer. When cooked, drain, steam-dry for a moment over low heat, and serve hot, sprinkled with chopped parsley.

For mashed potatoes, use:

2 lb potatoes 1 oz butter *or* margarine Chopped parsley	A little milk Salt and pepper Grated nutmeg

Prepare and cook peeled potatoes as for Boiled Potatoes, pass them through a sieve, or through a potato masher, or mash with a fork. Melt the fat (in one corner of the pan if the potatoes have been mashed in the pan itself) and beat in the potatoes. Add milk gradually and beat well until the mixture is thoroughly hot, and smooth. Season well and add a little grated nutmeg. Serve in a hot dish. Sprinkle with chopped parsley.

Successful mashed potato depends upon the use of a floury type of potato, thorough drying of the potatoes after the water has been strained off them, and the thorough mashing of the potatoes before the fat and milk are added.

For creamed potatoes, add 1 tablesp cream (single or double) to mashed potatoes.

For potato balls or croquettes, mix 1 lb mashed potatoes with 1 oz butter and 1 beaten egg. Season well with salt and pepper. Form into small balls or rolls. Coat twice with egg and crumbs and fry in deep fat at 190° C, 375 °F, for 4–5 min. Drain well and serve at once. If wanted for a garnish, re-heat

briefly, in the oven or by plunging into deep hot fat.

6 helpings

POTATO CHIPS AND POTATO STRAWS

6 medium-sized potatoes	Deep fat Salt

Scrub and rinse the potatoes. Peel them thinly. For chips—cut into sticks about 2 in long and $\frac{1}{2}$ in wide and thick. For straws—cut into strips the size of a wooden match. Drop them into cold water as they are cut. Rinse and drain and dry in a clean cloth. Put them into the frying-basket and lower them gently into hot deep fat at 180 °C, 360 °F. (Keep the heat fairly high as the potatoes will have cooled the fat.) When the potatoes are soft but *not* brown—about 3 min for chips and 1 min for straws—lift out the basket and heat the fat to 190 °C, 375 °F. Put back the basket and leave in the fat until the potatoes are crisp and golden brown—about 3 min for chips and 2 min for straws. Drain on absorbent paper, sprinkle with salt and serve immediately.

If potato chips or straws are to be served with any other fried dish, the second frying of the potatoes to brown and crisp them should be done after the other is fried. In this way the potatoes will be sent to table in their best condition.

6 helpings
> **Cooking time for chips, about 6 min**
> **for straws, about 3 min**

ROAST POTATOES

2 lb even-sized potatoes	Salt and pepper Dripping

Peel the potatoes and cut in halves or even in quarters if very large. Parboil and strain off the water and dry the potatoes over a low heat. Put into hot dripping in a roasting tin, or in the tin containing the roast joint. Roll the potatoes in the fat and cook till tender and brown.

> **Cooking time, to parboil, 10 min;**
> **to bake, 1 hr (approx)**

SAUTÉED OR TOSSED POTATOES

6 medium-sized potatoes (waxy ones)	1–2 oz butter *or* margarine Seasoning

Cook the potatoes, preferably in their skins, until only just soft. Let them dry thoroughly then peel and slice them $\frac{1}{4}$ in thick. Heat the fat in a frying-pan and put in the potatoes. Season them with salt and pepper. Toss in the fat until they are light brown and have absorbed all the fat. Serve at once.

4–6 helpings

BAKED TOMATOES

6 tomatoes A little butter *or* margarine Salt and pepper Castor sugar	Finely chopped tarragon (optional) Browned breadcrumbs (optional)

Wash the tomatoes and cut them in halves. Put them in a greased, deep fireproof dish. Season and sprinkle each with a pinch of sugar and a pinch of chopped tarragon, if used. Put a tiny piece of butter on each or cover with a well greased paper. Bake in a moderate oven (180 °C, 350 °F, Gas 4) until soft—about 20 min.

Alternatively, cut the tomatoes in half horizontally or make crossways cuts in the top of each. Press the cut portion into browned breadcrumbs before baking and top with the butter or margarine.

6 helpings

FRIED OR GRILLED TOMATOES

6 large tomatoes Butter *or* margarine *or*	bacon fat for frying Salt and pepper

Wash the tomatoes and cut in halves. Fry in hot fat, turning them once during frying. Season. Serve hot.

To grill tomatoes prepare as for fried tomatoes. Season and brush with melted

Boiled new potatoes

fat. Cook under a fairly hot grill, turning them once. Serve hot with bacon, sausages, fish dishes and all grilled meats.

6 helpings

MAIN COURSE VEGETABLE DISHES

CAULIFLOWER WITH CHEESE

1 large cauliflower $\frac{3}{4}$ pt cheese sauce Salt 1 heaped tablesp grated cheese	(dry Cheddar) *or* 1 dessertsp grated Cheddar cheese and 1 dessertsp grated Parmesan cheese

Cook the cauliflower as in the recipe for boiled cauliflower; drain well and dish up in a fireproof dish. Coat with thick cheese sauce. Sprinkle with grated cheese and immediately brown under a hot grill or in the top of a hot oven (220 °C, 425 °F, Gas 7). Serve at once before the cheese becomes 'tacky'.

Other vegetables can be cooked in the same way. Celery, leeks and onions are particularly good as main-course dishes when cooked with cheese.

BOILED OR BAKED CORN ON THE COB

6 ears *or* cobs of corn	Seasoning Butter

Remove the outer husks of the corn. Open the tender, pale green inner husks and take away all the silk surrounding the corn. Replace the inner husk and tie securely; place the ears in a saucepan with sufficient boiling water to cover them. Simmer gently 15–20 min. Drain and remove strings and husks. Serve with melted, seasoned butter. The flavour is best if the corn is nibbled from the cob with the teeth, each guest being supplied with melted butter in which to dip the corn.

For baked corn, remove husks and silk of the corn. Place in a roasting dish, cover with milk and bake at 190 °C, 375 °F, Gas 5 for about 45 min. Toss in 2 oz melted butter and place under a hot grill for a few minutes before serving.

6 helpings

STUFFED PEPPERS

6 small *or* 3 large peppers 1 tablesp breadcrumbs (optional)	A little melted butter *or* margarine (optional)

Stuffing

1 oz butter 1 oz flour $\frac{1}{2}$ pt milk, warmed Salt and freshly ground black pepper	1 green pepper, de-seeded and finely chopped 1 large cooking apple, peeled, cored and chopped $\frac{1}{4}$ lb grated Gruyère cheese

Wash and parboil the peppers. Drain, cut in half lengthways and remove seeds. Prepare the stuffing. Melt the butter, and add the flour. Cook gently for a few minutes. Add the milk slowly, and season to taste. Cook for a further 2–3 min until sauce thickens slightly. Add the apple, chopped pepper and cheese, and re-season if required. Fill the halved peppers with this stuffing, sprinkle with a few breadcrumbs and a little melted fat if desired. Put the stuffed peppers in a greased baking dish or on a baking sheet, and bake for 30 min at 150 °C, 300 °F, Gas 1–2.

6 helpings

VEGETABLE PIE

Short crust pastry, using

3 oz lard *or* vegetable fat	6 oz plain flour Water to mix

Filling

$\frac{3}{4}$ lb mushrooms 1 lb tomatoes	1 lb leeks Salt and pepper

Make the pastry and set it aside to rest while preparing the filling.

Wash and slice the mushrooms. Skin the tomatoes, quarter and remove seeds. Clean and slice the white ends of the leeks. Arrange the vegetables in a dish, seasoning well with salt and pepper. (Sliced peeled potatoes may also be added.) Cover with pastry, seal edges and cut vents to allow steam to escape. Cook in the centre of the oven at 190 °C, 375 °F, Gas 5 until crust is brown. The tomatoes and mushrooms will provide their own juice.

4 helpings

SALADS

APPLES, BANANA AND NUT SALAD

6 small rosy apples	2 bananas
4 lettuce leaves	Salad dressing
1 tablesp coarsely chopped nuts	Watercress *or* fine cress

Wash and dry the apples; cut a small piece off the top of each, and carefully scoop out most of the inside with a teaspoon. Shred the lettuce leaves and mix very lightly with nuts, sliced banana, a little of the apple pulp (chopped), and salad dressing. Fill the polished apple cases with the mixture. Serve on individual plates, decorating each with watercress or tiny bunches of fine cress.

6 helpings

BEETROOT SALAD

2 cooked beetroots
French dressing
Grated horseradish

Slice or dice the beetroot and arrange neatly. Baste with French dressing, after sprinkling with freshly grated horseradish. Dry mustard may be added to the French dressing and the horseradish omitted.

For a more elaborate salad, add 2 peeled, cored and diced dessert apples, 2 oz shelled walnuts and 1 large celery heart, diced. Garnish with watercress.

6 helpings

CARROT SALAD

3 large carrots	Finely chopped parsley
1 lettuce	
French dressing	

Grate the carrots finely and serve on a bed of lettuce leaves. Sprinkle with the French dressing. Garnish with chopped parsley.

Grated, raw carrot can be used with success in many salads. It should be grated very finely to be digestible, and sprinkled with lemon juice or French dressing as soon as grated to retain its bright colour.

6 helpings

CUCUMBER SALAD

1 large cucumber	Chopped parsley
Salt	Chopped tarragon
French dressing	

Slice the cucumber. Put on a plate and sprinkle with salt. Tilt the plate slightly so that the water may drain off easily and leave for $\frac{1}{2}$ hr. Rinse quickly in a colander and drain. Dish and pour over the French dressing. Sprinkle with parsley and tarragon.

6 helpings

LETTUCE SALAD

Lettuce, of the cabbage or cos variety, prepared correctly and dressed with a French dressing *or* Vinaigrette Sauce, provides the finest of all salads.

To prepare lettuce, cut off the stump of the lettuce and discard the coarse outer leaves only. Separate all leaves and wash them leaf by leaf under running water if possible, otherwise in several waters in a basin. Put into a salad shaker or a clean tea-towel and swing them to shake out the water. Leave to drain. If possible put into a covered box *or* into a casserole with a lid in the refrigerator for at least $\frac{1}{2}$ hr before dressing them for table.

The salads in which lettuce is used as a foundation are so numerous that it is unnecessary to name them all here.

POTATO SALAD

6 large new potatoes *or* waxy old potatoes	1 teasp chopped mint
French dressing	1 teasp chopped chives *or* spring onion
2 heaped tablesp chopped parsley	Salt and pepper

Cook the potatoes until just soft, in their

skins. Peel and cut into dice while still hot. Mix while hot with the dressing and the herbs and a little seasoning. Serve cold.

6 helpings

TOMATO SALAD

6 large firm tomatoes	**Finely chopped parsley**
Salt and pepper	
French dressing *or* **cream salad dressing**	

Skin and slice the tomatoes. Season lightly. Pour the dressing over the tomatoes. Sprinkle with chopped parsley.

6 helpings

top left: Apples filled with banana and nut salad

top right: Vegetable pie

below: Stuffed peppers

bottom right: Boiled Corn on the Cob

Puddings, Desserts and Ices

LARGE GRAIN MILK PUDDINGS
(Sago, whole rice, flaked tapioca or rice)

4 oz grain, any type above	$\frac{1}{2}$ oz finely shredded suet *or* butter
2 pt milk	
2–3 oz sugar	Grated nutmeg *or* similar flavouring

Grease a pie-dish. Wash the grain in cold water if required, and put it into the dish with the milk. Leave to stand for $\frac{1}{2}$ hr. Add the sugar, flake on the fat if used, and sprinkle on the flavouring. Bake very slowly (150 °C, 310 °F, Gas 2) until the pudding is thick and creamy, and brown on top, a minimum of 2–2$\frac{1}{2}$ hr. (The pudding is better if it cooks even more slowly, for 4–5 hr.)

Note 1 If a flavouring essence is used, it is mixed into the milk before cooking. **2** If dried or canned milk is used, reduce the amount of rice to 3 oz, use the amount of milk product which makes up to 1$\frac{3}{4}$ pt, and cook at 140° C, 275 °F, Gas $\frac{1}{2}$ for at least 3$\frac{1}{2}$–4 hr.

4–6 helpings

LARGE GRAIN MILK PUDDINGS WITH EGGS

4 oz large grain, any type	2–4 eggs
	2–3 oz sugar
2 pt milk	Flavouring

Wash the grain in cold water if necessary. Put the grain and milk into a strong or double saucepan, and cook slowly until the grain is tender. Remove from the heat, and allow to cool slightly. Separate the eggs and whisk the whites stiffly. Stir into the pudding the slightly beaten egg yolks, sugar and flavouring, and, lastly, fold in the whisked whites. Pour into a well-buttered pie-dish and bake in a warm oven (170 °C, 335 °F, Gas 3) for about 40 min, until the top is brown.

6 helpings

MEDIUM AND SMALL GRAIN MILK PUDDINGS
(Semolina, ground rice, small sago, crushed tapioca)

2 pt milk	3 oz grain, any type above
Flavouring	
	2–3 oz sugar

Heat the milk and infuse a stick or peel flavouring if used for about 10 min. Remove the flavouring.

Sprinkle the grain into the milk, stirring quickly to prevent lumps forming. Place over heat, and continue stirring while the milk simmers, until the grain is transparent and cooked through; this takes about 15 min. Add the sugar and any flavouring essence used.

The pudding can then be served as it is, hot or cold, or can be poured into a well-buttered pie-dish and baked in a moderate oven (180 °C, 350 °F, Gas 4) for 20–30 min until the top has browned.

6 helpings

MEDIUM AND SMALL GRAIN MILK PUDDINGS WITH EGGS

2 pt milk	**2–4 eggs**
Flavouring	**2–3 oz sugar**
3 oz grain, any	
type in previous	
recipe	

See Large Grain Milk Puddings.

6 helpings

FLAVOURINGS FOR ALL MILK AND CUSTARD PUDDINGS

Flavourings may be

1 Powdered or grated, e.g. ground cinnamon, grated lemon peel

2 In plant form, e.g. bay leaf

3 Concentrated, e.g. essences, various liqueurs

4 Liquid, e.g. lemon juice, wine

Powdered or grated flavourings are usually sifted into other dry ingredients or are sprinkled into, or on top of, liquid ones.

Leaf, stem and root flavourings can be infused in the liquid to be flavoured, e.g. in milk; or they may be included in a dish while it cooks, and removed before serving.

Concentrated essences and fruit juices are usually added to a dish or sauce shortly before completing it; in the case of liqueurs, the alcohol is driven off if, for instance, it is overheated or heated for long. Some liqueured dishes are flambéed or flamed, the alcohol being poured over the dish and set alight, to give a distinctive flavour.

CUSTARDS AND CUSTARD MIXTURES

Basically these are made from a mixture of eggs, milk and sugar, cooked very slowly until the mixture is just set. Custards can be cooked by 'boiling' (that is, by poaching) or by baking or steaming; but they must always be cooked very carefully and slowly since overcooking will make the mixture curdle. A custard which is to be unmoulded needs at least four eggs to one pt liquid or it is liable to break.

Pouring custards These are made by heating the mixture, and keeping it at a temperature *below* boiling point until the eggs are cooked evenly throughout. Doing this in a double boiler lessens the risk of curdling.

Baked custards The dish to contain the custard should be well greased. When filled, it should be placed in a tray of warm water. Bake slowly at about 170 °C, 325 °F, Gas 3 until the custard is set. Take it out of the water at once to prevent further cooking.

Steamed custards The basin must be well greased, and the custard covered with greased paper to prevent dripping condensed steam falling into it. Only a very gentle flow of steam should be allowed.

Flavourings Any of the flavourings suggested for milk puddings can be used.

BAKED OR STEAMED CUSTARD

1½ pt milk	**3–4 eggs for a**
Flavouring	**baked custard,**
Wine sauce	**plus 1 more for a**
1–1½ oz castor	**steamed custard**
sugar	

Beat the eggs with the sugar. Warm the milk and flavouring, and add gradually to the egg mixture, stirring well. Pour the mixture into a greased pie-dish for a baked custard or a buttered mould for a steamed one. Stand the pie-dish in a tray of warm water and bake in a warm oven (170 °C, 325–335 °F, Gas 3) for about 50 min. For a steamed custard, cover the mould with greased paper, secure it firmly, and steam gently for about 40 min until the custard is set in the centre. Turn out and serve with wine sauce.

5–6 helpings

BREAD AND BUTTER PUDDING

6 thin slices of bread and butter	3 eggs
2 oz sultanas *or* currants *or* stoned raisins *or* chopped candied peel	1½ oz sugar
	1½ pt milk

Grease a 2-pt pie-dish. Remove the bread crusts if you wish. Then cut the bread into squares or triangles, and lay them neatly in the dish. Sprinkle fruit over each layer. Beat the eggs with the sugar, add the milk and pour the mixture over the bread. It should only half fill the dish. Leave to soak for at least 30 min. Then bake for about 1 hr in a moderate oven (180 °C, 350 °F, Gas 4) until the custard is set.

5–6 helpings

QUEEN OF PUDDINGS

1 pt milk	2 oz granulated sugar
½ pt breadcrumbs	
2 oz butter *or* margarine	2 eggs
Grated rind of 2 lemons	3 tablesp jam
	2–4 oz castor sugar

Heat the milk and add the breadcrumbs, fat, lemon rind and granulated sugar. Leave to soak for 30 min. Separate the eggs, and stir the yolks into the milk mixture. Pour the mixture into a buttered pie-dish, and bake for about ¾ hr in a moderate oven (180 °C, 350 °F, Gas 4) until set. Now spread the jam on the pudding. Whip the egg whites very stiffly, sprinkle with 1 oz castor sugar and whip again until stiff. Then fold in lightly the rest of the sugar. Spread the meringue over the pudding, and put into a very cool oven (130 °C, 265 °F, Gas ½) until the top is set and golden-brown.

5–6 helpings

HOT SOUFFLÉS

Soufflés are flavoured starchy or fruit purées. They depend for their lightness on the air whisked into the egg whites which they contain. They must not get wet, or be jolted to knock the air out, and they should be served immediately they are removed from the cooking heat, as they fall as soon as they are cooled.

General hints

1 Before making a soufflé, prepare the tin or mould (see below) and see that the steamer or oven is on.

2 When making, whisk the egg whites very stiff, incorporating as much bulk of air as possible by lifting the fork or whisk in a rotating movement. Fold them into the soufflé very carefully. Cook straight away.

3 Time the preparation and cooking so that the soufflé *can* be served as soon as it is cooked.

To prepare the tin or mould Grease with clarified butter or tasteless cooking fat. Tie a double band of greaseproof paper or aluminium foil round the container, which rises 3 in above the top. (The cut edge of paper should be at the top.) For a steamed soufflé, cut a circle of greaseproof paper for the top of the tin to prevent water dripping on to the soufflé.

Steamed soufflés These are cooked in a steamer or saucepan containing enough boiling water to come half-way up the sides of the pan. Stand the soufflé tin on an upturned saucer or plate so that it does not touch the bottom of the pan itself. Only half fill the mould. Steam gently but steadily, avoiding jolting the pan. The soufflé is cooked when it is just risen and firm to the touch. Turn out on to a hot dish, and serve at once.

Baked soufflés These are served in the cooking dish, usually a large charlotte or soufflé mould, or in individual ovenproof dishes. The greased dish should not be more than ¾ full. Avoid opening the oven door during cooking, so that no cold draught or jolting can make the soufflé sink. When cooked, it should be well risen and firm.

96

CHOCOLATE SOUFFLÉ

2 oz finely grated　　**½ teasp vanilla**
plain chocolate　　　**essence**
⅜ pt milk　　　　　　**5 egg whites**
1 oz butter
1½ oz plain flour
4 egg yolks
3 oz castor sugar

Prepare a soufflé tin or mould. Dissolve the chocolate in the milk. Melt the butter, add the flour and let it cook for a few minutes without colouring. Add the milk and beat well until smooth. Reheat until the mixture thickens and comes away from the sides of the pan. Allow to cool slightly. Beat in the egg yolks well, one at a time, add the sugar and vanilla essence. Whisk the egg whites stiffly and fold them lightly into the mixture. Turn into the mould; cover, and steam very gently for about 1 hr.

6 helpings

BATTER PUDDING, BAKED OR STEAMED

½ lb plain flour　　　**1 pt milk**
¼ teasp each　　　　**1 tablesp cooking**
sugar and salt　　　　**fat or lard**
2 eggs　　　　　　　　**Wine _or_ jam sauce**

Sift the flour, sugar and salt into a basin. Make a well in the centre of the flour and break the eggs into this. Add about a gill of the milk. Stir, gradually working the flour down from the sides and adding more milk, as required, to make a stiff batter consistency. Beat well for about 5 min. Add the rest of the milk. Cover and leave to stand for 30 min if desired.

Put the fat into a Yorkshire pudding tin and heat in the oven until hot. The fat should just be beginning to smoke. Quickly pour in the batter and leave to cook in a hot oven (220 °C, 425 °F, Gas 7) at the top of the oven until nicely browned. Reduce the heat to 190 °C, 375 °F, Gas 5, and finish cooking through for 10–15 min. Serve with wine or jam sauce.

For a steamed Batter Pudding, prepare the same mixture. Pour it into a well-greased pudding basin. Cover with greased paper and steam for 2 hr.

6 helpings

PANCAKES

Batter as for	1 lemon
Batter Pudding	Castor sugar
above	
A little cooking	
fat	

Put about $\frac{1}{4}$ oz of cooking fat into a cleaned frying pan and heat until it is just beginning to smoke. Quickly pour in enough batter to coat thinly the bottom of the pan, tilting the pan to make sure that the batter runs over evenly. Move the frying pan over a quick heat until the pancake is set and browned underneath. Make sure that the pancake is loose at the sides, then toss, or turn with a broad bladed knife or fish slice. Brown on the other side and turn on to a sugared paper. Sprinkle with sugar and lemon juice, roll up and keep hot while cooking the rest. Serve dredged with castor sugar and pieces of cut lemon.

Other flavourings such as apple, jam, orange, tangerine or brandy may be used, as follows:

Apple pancakes Add grated lemon rind to the batter. Fill with apple purée mixed with seedless raisins and a little lemon juice.

Jam pancakes Spread with jam before rolling up.

Orange pancakes Make the pancakes but sprinkle with orange juice and serve with pieces of cut orange.

Tangerine pancakes Add grated tangerine rind to the batter. Sprinkle with tangerine juice before rolling up.

Brandy filling for pancakes Cream together 2 oz butter and 1 oz castor sugar until soft. Work in 1 tablesp brandy and 1 teasp lemon juice. Spread the pancakes with this mixture. Roll up and put immediately into the serving dish.

SWEET FRITTER COATING BATTERS
Light

2 oz plain flour	$\frac{1}{2}$ gill warm water
Pinch each of	1 egg white
sugar and salt	
1 dessertsp salad	
oil *or* oiled butter	

Sift together the flour and salt. Mix to a smooth consistency with the oil and water. Beat well, and leave to stand for 30 min. Just before using, whisk the egg white stiffly and fold it into the batter.

Rich

4 oz plain flour	1 egg
Pinch each of	1 gill milk
sugar and of salt	

Sift together the flour and salt. Make a well in the centre of the flour and add the egg and some of the milk. Mix to a stiff consistency, using more milk if required. Beat well. Add the rest of the milk. Leave to stand for about 30 min.

CHRISTMAS PUDDING
(Rich, boiled)

10 oz sultanas	$\frac{1}{2}$ lb breadcrumbs
10 oz currants	10 oz finely
$\frac{1}{2}$ lb raisins	chopped *or*
2 oz sweet	shredded suet
almonds (skinned	6 eggs
and chopped)	$\frac{1}{4}$ gill stout
1 level teasp	Juice of 1 orange
ground ginger	1 wineglass
$\frac{1}{2}$ lb plain flour	brandy
Pinch of salt	$\frac{1}{2}$ pt milk
1 lb soft brown	(approx)
sugar	
$\frac{1}{2}$ lb mixed finely	
chopped candied	
peel	
1 level teasp	
mixed spice	
1 level teasp	
grated nutmeg	

Grease three 1 pt pudding basins. Prepare the dried fruit; stone and chop the raisins; chop the nuts.

Sift the flour, salt, spice, ginger and nutmeg into a mixing bowl. Add the sugar, breadcrumbs, suet, fruit, nuts and candied peel. Beat the eggs well and add to them the stout, orange juice and brandy, and stir this into the dry ingredients adding enough milk to make the mixture of a soft dropping consistency. Put the mixture into prepared basins. Cover and boil steadily for 6–7 hr. Take the puddings out of the water and cover them with a clean dry cloth and, when cold, store in a cool place until required.

When required, boil the puddings for $1\frac{1}{2}$ hr before serving.

3 puddings (each to give 6 medium helpings)

CHRISTMAS PUDDING
(Economical, boiled or steamed)

1 apple	6 oz mixed
1 lb mixed dried	chopped candied
fruit (sultanas,	peel
currants, raisins)	Juice and rind of
4 oz plain flour	1 lemon
1 oz self-raising	2 eggs
flour	Milk to mix
Pinch of salt	A little caramel *or*
4 oz breadcrumbs	gravy browning
4 oz soft brown	A few drops of
sugar	almond essence
$\frac{1}{2}$ lb shredded suet	

Grease two small basins or one large basin; peel, core and chop the apple; prepare the dried fruit. Sift together the plain flour, self-raising flour and salt into a mixing bowl. Add the breadcrumbs, dried fruit, sugar, suet, candied peel and grated lemon rind. Beat the eggs and milk together and stir them into the dry ingredients with the lemon juice, adding more milk to make the mixture of a soft dropping consistency. Add a little caramel *or* gravy browning to darken the mixture slightly (about a level teasp), and the almond essence. Mix well in. Turn into the basin, cover and boil for 4 hr or steam for 5 hr.

12 helpings

FRUIT PUDDING WITH SUET CRUST

1–$1\frac{1}{2}$ lb fresh	2–3 oz granulated
fruit	sugar

Suet crust pastry

$\frac{1}{2}$ lb plain flour	Pinch of salt
1 teasp baking	3 oz finely
powder	chopped suet

Fillings

Apples	Damsons
Blackberries and	Gooseberries
apples	Plums
Blackcurrants	

Sift the flour and baking powder, add the suet and salt. Mix with sufficient water to make a soft, but firm, dough. Grease and line a basin (*see below*). Fill to the top with the fruit and sugar and add $\frac{1}{4}$ gill of cold water. Put on the top crust.

To boil Cover over with a well-floured cloth and boil for $2\frac{1}{2}$–3 hr.

To steam Cover with greased paper and steam for $2\frac{1}{2}$–3 hr.

To line the basin Cut off $\frac{1}{4}$ of the pastry for the top. Roll the remaining pastry $\frac{1}{2}$ in larger than the top of the basin, drop the pastry into the greased basin, and with the fingers work the pastry evenly up the sides to the top. Roll out the lid to the size of the top of the basin, wet the edges and secure it firmly round the inside of the pastry.

6 helpings

LEMON PUDDING

6 oz flour	2 oz sugar
Pinch of salt	Juice and rind
1 rounded teasp	of 1 lemon
baking powder	1 egg
2 oz butter *or*	Milk to mix
margarine	

Grease a $1\frac{1}{2}$ pt pudding basin. Sift together the flour, salt and baking powder. Rub in the fat and add the sugar and grated lemon rind. Mix to a soft dropping consistency with

the beaten egg, lemon juice and milk. Put the pudding into the greased basin and cover with a piece of greased paper. Steam for $1\frac{1}{2}$–2 hr.

For a steamed jam pudding, substitute vanilla essence for lemon juice. Put 1 tablesp red jam in the basin before the mixture, and serve a hot jam sauce with the pudding.

4–6 helpings

TREACLE LAYER PUDDING

2 oz breadcrumbs
Rind of 1 lemon
$\frac{1}{2}$ lb treacle *or*
golden syrup
(approx)

Suet crust pastry, rich

left: Apple pancakes   top: Christmas pudding

4–6 oz finely chopped *or* shredded suet	Pinch of salt
	2 rounded teasp baking powder
12 oz plain flour	Water to mix

Sift flour, salt and baking powder and mix with suet and sufficient water to make a

soft, but firm, dough. Divide the dough into two equal portions, using one portion to line a 2 pt basin. From the other portion cut off enough to make the lid; roll out the remainder thinly.

Mix the breadcrumbs and grated lemon rind.

Put a layer of treacle in the basin; sprinkle well with the breadcrumbs. Cover with a round of the thinly-rolled pastry. Moisten the edge of it with water and join securely to the pastry at the side of the basin. Add another layer of treacle, crumbs and pastry; then more treacle and crumbs. Finally cover with the rolled-out top as the last layer of pastry. Cover with greased paper. Steam for $2\frac{1}{2}$ hr.

6–7 helpings

APPLE CHARLOTTE

2 lb cooking apples	8 thinly-cut slices of bread and butter
4 oz brown sugar	
Grated rind and juice of 1 lemon	Castor sugar

Grease a 2 pt charlotte mould with butter. Peel, core and slice the apples. Place a layer in the bottom of the mould and sprinkle with sugar, grated lemon rind and lemon juice. Cover with thin slices of bread and butter. Repeat until the dish is full, finishing with a layer of bread and butter. Cover with greased paper. Bake in a moderate oven (180 °C, 350 °F, Gas 4) for $\frac{3}{4}$–1 hr. Turn out of the dish, if desired, and dredge well with castor sugar before serving.

Alternatively, cut the bread $\frac{1}{4}$ in thick before buttering it; line the mould with it, buttered side outward, so that the pieces fit tightly together. Fill with the remaining ingredients packed tightly, and bake as above.

5–6 helpings

APPLE OR OTHER FRUIT CRUMBLE

$1\frac{1}{2}$ lb apples	6 oz plain flour
4 oz brown sugar	3 oz castor sugar
A little grated lemon rind	$\frac{1}{4}$ teasp ground ginger
$\frac{1}{2}$ gill water (approx)	
3 oz butter *or* margarine	

Peel, core and slice the apples into a pan. Add $\frac{1}{2}$ gill water, 4 oz brown sugar and lemon rind. Cook gently with lid on the pan until soft. Place in a greased 2 pt pie-dish. Rub the fat into the flour until the consistency of fine breadcrumbs. Add the castor sugar, ground ginger and mix well. Sprinkle the crumble over the apple; press down lightly. Bake in a moderate oven (180 °C, 350 °F, Gas 4) until the crumble is golden-brown, and the apples are cooked; this takes about 30–40 min, depending on the cooking quality of the apples. Dredge with castor sugar and serve with custard *or* cream.

For apples the same weight of the following may be substituted: damsons, gooseberries, pears, plums, raspberries *or* rhubarb, and the crumble named accordingly.

6 helpings

BAKED APPLES OR APPLE DUMPLINGS

6 cooking apples	$\frac{1}{2}$ gill water
2 oz Demerara sugar	Pastry (optional)

Fillings

1	2 oz moist sugar and 2 oz butter	3	3 oz stoned dates *or* sultanas *or* currants *or* raisins, 2 oz soft brown sugar and 1 teasp ground cinnamon
2	Blackcurrant *or* raspberry *or* strawberry *or* apricot jam		

Prepare the filling. Wash and core the apples. Cut round the skin of each apple with the tip of a sharp knife, $\frac{2}{3}$ of the way up from the base. Put the apples into a fireproof dish and fill the centres with the chosen filling. Sprinkle with the Demerara sugar. Add the water. Bake in a moderate oven (180 °C, 350 °F, Gas 4) until the apples are soft in the centre—about $\frac{3}{4}$–1 hr depending on the cooking quality of the apples.

Baked apple dumplings Stuff the apples after peeling and coring them. Use 12 oz short crust pastry if they are big apples, 8 oz if they are small. Cut the pastry into 6 pieces, and roll out in rounds. Work a piece of pastry round each apple, and seal with a little water. Place the dumplings, join side down, on a greased baking sheet. Brush with milk, dredge with castor sugar and bake at 200 °C, 400 °F, Gas 6 for about 30 min. Test with a skewer whether the apples are soft. If not, reduce heat to 150 °C, 300 °F, Gas 2 and bake a little longer.

6 helpings

APPLE PIE

Short crust	4 oz moist
pastry, frozen	sugar
or using 6 oz	4 cloves *or*
flour, etc.	½ teasp grated
1½–2 lb apples	lemon rind

Peel, quarter and core the apples and cut in thick slices. Place half the apples in a 1½ pt pie dish, add the sugar and flavouring and pile the remaining fruit on top, piling it high in the centre. Line the edge of the pie dish and cover. Knock up the edges of the pastry with the back of a knife. Bake for 40 min, first in a fairly hot oven (200 °C, 400 °F, Gas 6), reducing the heat to moderate (180 °C, 350 °F, Gas 4) when the pastry is set. Dredge with castor sugar and serve hot or cold.

If you wish, brush the pastry with egg white and sprinkle with sugar before cooking.

6 helpings

FRUIT FLAN OR TART

Rich shortcrust pastry, using 4 oz flour, etc

Filling

1 medium-sized can of fruit *or* ¾ lb fresh fruit, e.g. apples, strawberries, pears, pineapple, cherries, apricots, peaches, plums, etc or dried fruit such as apple slices, apricots and prunes, well soaked

Coating glaze

¼ pt syrup from	Sugar (if	Lemon juice to
canned fruit, or	necessary)	taste
fruit juice, *or*	1 teasp arrowroot	
water		

Decoration (optional)

Whipped sweetened cream

Line a 7-in flan ring or tart plate with the pastry. Prick the bottom and bake it 'blind'. Bake for about 20 min first in a fairly hot oven (200 °C, 400 °F, Gas 6), then reducing the heat as the pastry sets to moderate (180 °C, 350 °F, Gas 4). When the pastry is cooked, remove the paper and filling used for 'blind' baking and replace the case in the oven for 5 min to dry the bottom. Allow to cool.

If fresh or dried fruit is used, stew gently till tender, if necessary. Drain the fruit. Place the sugar if used and the liquid in a pan and boil for 10 min. Blend the arrowroot with some lemon juice and add it to the syrup, stirring all the time. Continue stirring, cook for 3 min then cool slightly. Arrange the fruit attractively in the flan case and coat it with fruit syrup. Serve cold.

If liked, a flan can be decorated with piped whipped, sweetened cream.

For a quick flan or tart case, a crumb crust or cake mixture from a packet can be used satisfactorily.

In some areas, apple flans or tarts are given a crumbled cheese topping instead of fruit syrup.

LEMON MERINGUE PIE

Rich shortcrust pastry, using 8 oz flour, etc

Filling

2 eggs	2 oz castor sugar
8 oz can	2 level teasp
sweetened	cream of tartar
condensed milk	1 lemon

Make the pastry and line an 8- or 9-in pie plate. Bake it 'blind'.

To make the filling Separate the egg yolks from the whites. Beat the yolks until thick and lemon coloured. Fold in the condensed milk, lemon rind, juice and cream of tartar. Pour into the baked pie shell. Spread with meringue made from the egg whites and the sugar. Decorate lightly with cherries and angelica. Bake in a cool oven (100 °C, 200 °F, Gas $\frac{1}{2}$) for $\frac{1}{2}$–1 hr. Serve cold.

ITALIAN BAVAROIS OR CREAM

1 lemon	$\frac{1}{2}$ oz gelatine
$\frac{1}{2}$ pt milk	$\frac{1}{2}$ gill water
3 egg yolks *or*	$\frac{1}{2}$ pt double
1 whole egg and	cream
1 yolk	
2–3 oz castor sugar	

Infuse thin strips of lemon rind in the milk. Beat eggs and sugar until liquid and make a thick pouring custard with the flavoured milk, straining back into the pan to cook and thicken. Allow to cool. Soak gelatine in the water for 5 min, then heat to dissolve. Stir juice of lemon gently into the cooled custard, and add the dissolved gelatine, stirring again as it cools. Whip the cream and fold lightly into the custard mixture just before setting.

Pour into a prepared mould and leave to set. If you like, the cream can be poured into individual glass dishes, and decorated according to your own taste.

6 helpings   **Setting time 1–2 hr**

VANILLA CREAM

Make like Italian Bavarois or Cream, but use vanilla essence instead of lemon rind and juice.

BASIC MILANAISE SOUFFLÉ

2 lemons	$\frac{1}{2}$ oz gelatine
3–4 eggs, according to size	$\frac{1}{4}$ pt water
	$\frac{1}{2}$ pt double cream
5 oz castor sugar	

Decoration

Chopped pistachio nuts

Wash lemons dry, and grate rind finely. Whisk the egg yolks, sugar, rind and lemon juice over hot water until thick and creamy, then remove bowl from the hot water and continue whisking until cool. Soften the gelatine in the $\frac{1}{4}$ pt water, and heat to dissolve. Half-whip the cream. Whisk the egg whites very stiffly. Add the gelatine, still hot, in a thin stream, to the egg mixture, and stir in as you do it. Fold in the cream and the stiffly-whipped whites. Fold the mixture very lightly until setting is imminent, when the mixture pulls against the spoon. Pour into the soufflé dish and leave to set. Remove the paper band by coaxing it away from the mixture with a knife dipped in hot water. Decorate the sides with chopped, blanched pistachio nuts, and the top with whipped cream, if liked.

This is a good 'basic' soufflé recipe. It can be flavoured and decorated with almost any flavouring and garnish, such as coffee, chocolate, fruit or a liqueur, with appropriate small sweets or nuts as decoration.

6 helpings   **Setting time 2 hr**

TRIFLE (TRADITIONAL)

4 individual sponge cakes	$\frac{1}{2}$ pt custard using $\frac{1}{2}$ pt milk,
Raspberry *or* strawberry jam	1 egg and 1 egg yolk
6 macaroons	$\frac{1}{2}$ 6-oz carton
12 miniature macaroons	double cream
$\frac{1}{4}$ pt sherry	1 egg white
Grated rind of $\frac{1}{2}$ lemon	1–2 oz castor sugar
1 oz almonds (blanched and shredded)	

Decoration

Glacé cherries	**Angelica**

Split the sponge cakes into two and spread the lower halves with jam. Replace tops. Arrange in a glass dish and cover with macaroons and miniatures. Soak with sherry, and sprinkle with lemon rind and almonds. Cover with the custard and leave to cool. Whisk the cream, egg white and sugar together until stiff and pile on top of the

Milanaise soufflé

Traditional trifle

trifle. Decorate with glacé cherries and angelica.

Fruit trifles, such as Apricot or Gooseberry, are made by substituting layers of puréed or chopped fruit for the jam.

6 helpings

MERINGUE TOPPING AND SHELLS

4 eggs	$\frac{1}{2}$ lb castor sugar

Meringue for topping fruit dishes may be required less sweet than the recipe below. If so, only half the sugar is whisked into the stiff foam. The mixture is then piled on the dessert, dusted lightly with castor sugar and baked in a cool oven (140 °C, 290 °F, Gas 1) for about 30–40 min.

Make sure that the egg whites are fresh and contain no trace of yolk or grease. Break down with a whisk to an even-textured liquid by tapping lightly for a few moments. Then whisk evenly and continuously until a firm, stiff, close-textured foam is obtained. Whisk in 1 tablesp of the sugar. Add the rest of the sugar, a little at a time, by folding it in lightly with a metal spoon.

For a single large meringue shell, make a circle in pencil on greaseproof paper. Cover the pencil line with a layer of meringue. Pipe a 'wall' of meringue round the edge with a forcing bag. (For small meringue shells, force through a $\frac{3}{8}$-in pipe into small rounds, *or* form into egg-shapes with two spoons, dipped in cold water, and place on strips of oiled kitchen paper on baking sheets.) Dredge well with castor sugar and dry in a cool oven (140 °C, 290 °F, Gas 1), placed low to avoid discolouring and reduce to 130 °C, 265 °F, Gas $\frac{1}{2}$ after 1 hr. If a pure white meringue is required, *very* slow drying is essential, by leaving the meringue in a barely warm oven overnight.

FRUIT PURÉES

Fruit purées for all sweet dishes including creams, ice creams and sauces are made by rubbing fresh, frozen or canned fruit through a fine sieve, or by using an electric blender. Fruit containing pips or stones must be sieved before blending. A nylon sieve should always be used as fruit is acid.

FRUIT SALAD

3 oz granulated sugar	6 oz green grapes
½ pt water	1 small can
3 oranges	pineapple
Rind and juice	segments
of 1 lemon	3 red-skinned
3 ripe dessert	dessert apples
pears	

Bring the sugar and water to the boil, together with strips of rind taken from 1 orange and the lemon. Cool. Sieve to remove the rind.

Cut up the oranges, removing the skin and white pith, and section out the flesh, removing the pips. Halve the grapes removing the pips. Place these in the cooled sugar and water. Empty the pineapple pieces and juice into the fruit salad. Refrigerate if possible.

Just before serving, quarter, core and slice the apples thinly and toss in the lemon juice. Dice the pears and toss in lemon juice also. Add these to the fruit salad. Arrange attractively in a suitable serving dish. Chill and serve.

Fresh pineapple and canned mandarin segments are attractively coloured fruit to use. Try piling the salad in a shell of half shell of pineapple.

BASIC ICE CREAM CUSTARDS

Economical

1 oz custard powder	1 pt milk
	4 oz castor sugar

Blend the custard powder with a little of the milk. Boil remaining milk and pour on to the blended mixture. Return to pan and simmer, stirring continuously. Add sugar; cover, and allow to cool when thick.

With eggs

1 pt milk	4 oz castor sugar
1 oz custard powder	3 eggs

Heat the milk. Beat together the eggs and sugar. Add the hot milk slowly, stirring continuously. Return to the pan and cook without boiling until custard coats the back of a wooden spoon. Strain, cover and cool.

BASIC (VANILLA) ICE CREAM

Economical

¼ pt cream *or* prepared evaporated milk (see above)	1 pt cold ice cream custard
	1 teasp vanilla essence

Half whip the cream or evaporated milk. Add the custard and vanilla. Chill and freeze.

6 helpings

Rich

¼ pt cream	1 teasp vanilla essence
½ pt cold ice cream custard	
½ oz castor sugar	

Half whip the cream. Add the custard, sugar and vanilla. Chill and freeze.

BURNT ALMOND ICE CREAM

2 oz loaf sugar	¾ gill cream
2 oz almonds	1 tablesp kirsch
1½ pt ice cream custard	(optional)

Blanch, shred and bake the almonds until brown. Put the sugar and a few drops of water in a saucepan and boil until it acquires a deep golden colour. Add the cream, boil up and stir into the custard. Chill, add almonds and kirsch, if used, and then freeze the mixture.

PEACH MELBA

4–5 firm, ripe peaches ½ gill Melba sauce Vanilla essence	4 oz sugar ½ pt vanilla ice cream, home-made *or* bought

Halve and peel the peaches. Add the vanilla to the syrup and dissolve in it the sugar. Poach the peaches in the syrup until tender but not broken. Lift out the peaches, drain them on a sieve, and allow to get thoroughly cold. Serve them piled around a mound of vanilla ice cream in a silver dish. Set this dish in another dish containing shaved ice. Pour over a rich raspberry syrup, which must be previously iced. Serve at once.

This is the original recipe created in honour of Dame Nellie Melba. It is now often made as follows:

1 pt vanilla ice cream 6 canned peach halves	½ pt Melba sauce ¼ pt sweetened whipped cream

Place a scoop or slice of ice cream in 6 sundae glasses. Cover with a peach half. Coat with Melba sauce. Pipe a large rose of cream on top of each.

Other fruits are also used. Pears dipped in lemon juice team well with raspberries, for instance.

6 individual glasses

MELBA SAUCE

To make Melba sauce pass the required quantity of fresh raspberries through a nylon sieve and sweeten with icing sugar. The sauce is not cooked. Use as required.

BANANA SPLIT

6 bananas 1 pt vanilla ice cream *or* 1 bought brick ½ pt Melba sauce ¼ pt sweetened whipped cream	2 oz chopped walnuts 8 maraschino cherries

Peel the bananas, split in half lengthways and place in small oval dishes. Place two small scoops or slices of ice cream between the halves of bananas. Coat the ice cream with melba sauce; sprinkle with whipped cream and cherries.

HAWAIIAN DREAMS

1 large can crushed pineapple ½ oz gelatine 2 teasp lemon juice 1 pt vanilla *or* chocolate ice cream	2 oz chopped browned almonds ¼ pt sweetened whipped cream 6–8 maraschino cherries

Measure the crushed pineapple and make it up to 1 pt with water. Dissolve the gelatine in a little of the liquid but do not allow to boil. Add it to the crushed pineapple with the lemon juice. Pour into individual glasses to set. Just before serving, place a scoop of ice cream on top of the set mixture. Sprinkle with nuts. Decorate with a rose of cream and place a cherry on top.

6 individual glasses

SYRUP FOR WATER ICES

2 lb loaf sugar	1 pt water

Place the sugar and water in a strong saucepan. Allow the sugar to dissolve over gentle heat. Do not stir. When the sugar has dissolved, gently boil the mixture for 10 min, or, if a saccharometer is available, until it registers about 100 °C, 220 °F. Remove scum as it rises. Strain, cool and store. Makes 1 pt syrup.

LEMON WATER ICE

6 lemons 2 oranges	1½ pt syrup, as above

Peel the fruit thinly and place the rind in a basin. Add the hot syrup, cover and cool. Add the juice of the lemons and oranges. Strain, chill and freeze.

6 helpings

Basic Recipes, Sauces and Trimmings

ANCHOVY BUTTER

Use 2 oz butter, and salt and pepper to taste, with these ingredients: 6 bottled anchovies, lemon juice to taste. Do not use salt.

ANCHOVY SAUCE

To $\frac{1}{2}$ pt basic white sauce (see below) made from fish stock *or* water *or* $\frac{1}{2}$ milk and $\frac{1}{2}$ water add 1 *or* 2 teasp anchovy essence to taste and a few drops lemon juice and a few drops of cochineal to tint the sauce a dull pink.

APPLE SAUCE

1 lb apples	Rind and juice of $\frac{1}{2}$
2 tablesp water	lemon
$\frac{1}{2}$ oz butter *or*	Sugar to taste
margarine	

Stew the apples very gently with the water, butter and lemon rind until they are pulpy. Beat them quite smooth or rub them through a hair or nylon sieve. Reheat the sauce with the lemon juice and sweeten to taste.

For Apple Raisin sauce, add $\frac{1}{2}$ tablesp chopped parsley and 1 oz seedless raisins before reheating.

ASPIC JELLY 1.

2 egg whites and shells	Bouquet garni (parsley, thyme, bay leaf)
1 lemon	10 peppercorns
2 chicken *or* beef bouillon cubes	1 teasp salt
1 qt water	
$2\frac{1}{2}$ oz gelatine	
$\frac{1}{4}$ pt malt vinegar	
1 tablesp tarragon vinegar	
1 onion	
1 carrot	
2–3 sticks of celery	

Whisk the egg whites slightly, wash the shells, peel the lemon rind as thinly as possible, and strain the juice; crumble the cubes. Put them with the rest of the ingredients into a pan, whisk over heat until boiling, then simmer very gently for about 20 min. Strain through a jelly bag.

This jelly is used principally for lining and garnishing moulds. If too stiff, it may be diluted with a little water, or sherry, when additional flavour is desired.

6 helpings

ASPIC JELLY 2.

1 qt jellied veal *or* fish stock	2 sticks of celery
1 oz gelatine	2 egg whites and shells
Bouquet garni (parsley, thyme, bay leaf)	1 glass sherry (optional)
	$\frac{1}{4}$ pt vinegar

Let the stock become quite cold, and remove every particle of fat. Put it into a stewpan with the gelatine, herbs, celery cut into large pieces, the egg whites previously slightly beaten and the shells previously washed and dried. Whisk over heat until nearly boiling, then add the wine and vinegar. Continue the whisking until quite boiling, then reduce the heat and simmer for about 10 min, strain till clear, and use.

BASIC BROWN SAUCE

1 small carrot	1 oz flour
1 onion	1 pt brown stock
1 oz dripping	Salt and pepper

Thinly slice the carrot and onion. Melt the dripping and fry the onion and carrot in it slowly until they are golden-brown. Stir in the flour and fry it even more slowly till it is also golden-brown. Stir in the stock, bring to simmering point, season, then simmer for $\frac{1}{2}$ hr. Strain the sauce before use. As the frying of the flour is a long process extra colour may be given to the sauce by adding a piece of brown onion skin, or a little gravy browning or a little meat or vegetable extract which will also add to the flavour.

Cooking time 40 min–1 hr

BASIC WHITE SAUCE
For a coating sauce

2 oz butter *or* margarine	vegetable to suit dish), *or* a mixture of stock and milk
2 oz flour	
Pinch of salt	
1 pt milk *or* stock (fish, meat *or*	

For a pouring sauce

1½ oz butter *or* margarine

1½ oz flour	for coating sauce
1 pt of liquid as	Pinch of salt

Melt the fat in a deep saucepan, large enough to hold the amount of liquid with just enough room to spare for beating the sauce. Stir the flour into the fat and allow it to bubble for 2–3 min over a gentle heat. On no account allow it to change colour; this is a white roux. Remove from heat and stir in $\frac{1}{2}$ the liquid gradually. Return to moderate heat and stir the sauce briskly until it thickens, then beat it vigorously. Season and use it at once. If the sauce must be kept hot, cover it with wet greaseproof paper and a lid, and before use beat it again in case skin or lumps have formed.

A coating sauce should coat the back of the wooden spoon used for stirring, and should only just settle to its own level in the pan.

A pouring sauce should barely mask the spoon; it should flow freely, and easily settle to its own level in the pan.

For Melted Butter sauce, whisk in 2 extra oz butter, a nut at a time, just before serving.

Cooking time 15 min

BÉCHAMEL SAUCE

1 pt milk	6 peppercorns
1 small onion	A small bunch of herbs
1 small carrot	
2 in celery stick	2 oz butter
1 bay leaf	2 oz flour
1 clove	$\frac{1}{8}$ pt cream (optional)
$\frac{1}{4}$ teasp mace	
Salt	

Warm the milk with the vegetables, herbs, salt and spices, and bring it slowly to simmering point. Put a lid on the pan and stand it in a warm place on the cooker to infuse for $\frac{1}{2}$ hr. Strain the milk, melt the butter, add the flour. Cook this roux for a few minutes without browning it. Stir the flavoured milk gradually into the roux. Bring the sauce to boiling point, stirring vigorously. If cream is used, add it to the sauce just at boiling point and do not reboil it.

Béchamel sauce can be made with $\frac{1}{2}$ white stock and $\frac{1}{2}$ milk; the result will have a good flavour but will be less creamy.

BEURRE MANIÉ

The most economical way to thicken gravies, sauces and soups is with beurre manié or butter and flour kneaded together, usually in equal amounts. Work these together until smoothly blended. Drop small nuts of the mixture, one by one, into the near-boiling liquid. Whisk the sauce until it boils, by which time the thickening should be smoothly blended in.

Beurre manié will keep for several weeks in the fridge.

BOILED LONG GRAIN RICE

8 oz long grain rice	Water to cover 1 teasp salt

Put rice, water and salt into a saucepan, bring to the boil and stir once. Lower heat so that the water only simmers. Cover and cook for 10–15 min, or until the water is absorbed.

To serve hot, rinse the rice under hot water and top with a few flakes of butter if desired. If wanted for a salad, rinse under cold water, cool, cover and chill.

BOUQUET GARNI or BUNCH OF FRESH HERBS or FAGGOT OF HERBS

1 sprig of thyme	1 small bay leaf
1 sprig of marjoram	A few stalks of parsley
1 small sage leaf (optional)	A few chives (optional)
1 strip of lemon rind (optional)	Sprig of chervil (optional)

Tie all the herbs into a bunch with thick cotton or fine string. Alternatively the herbs may be tied in a small square of muslin. Add to soups, stews, sauces, etc. while they cook.

BRANDY BUTTER

3 oz butter	1 teasp–1 tablesp brandy
6 oz icing sugar *or*	
4½ oz icing sugar and 1 oz ground almonds	1 whipped egg white (optional)

Cream the butter till soft. Sift the icing sugar and cream it with the butter till white and light in texture. Mix in the almonds if used. Work the brandy carefully into the mixture. Fold the stiffly whipped egg white into the sauce. Serve with Christmas or other steamed puddings.

This sauce may be stored for several weeks in an airtight jar. It makes an excellent filling for sweet sandwiches.

BREAD SAUCE

1 large onion	2 tablesp cream (optional)
2 cloves	
Pinch of ground mace	
1 bay leaf	
4 peppercorns	
1 allspice berry	
½ pt milk	
2 oz dry white breadcrumbs	
½ oz butter	
Salt and pepper	

Put the onion and spices into the milk, bring them very slowly to boiling point. Cover the pan and infuse over a gentle heat for ½–1 hr. Strain the liquid. To it add the crumbs and butter, and season to taste. Keep the mixture just below simmering point for 20 min. Stir in the cream if used, serve the sauce at once. Serve with roast chicken or turkey.

COURT BOUILLON

1 small carrot	Sprig of parsley
1 small onion	2 peppercorns
1 pt water	
1 dessertsp vinegar	
1 level teasp salt	
½ bay leaf	

Peel and slice the carrot and onion. Place all the ingredients for the court bouillon in a pan, bring to the boil and boil for 5 min, strain and return to the pan.

CROÛTES AND CROÛTONS

A croûte is a fried or toasted slice of bread (round, square, etc) used as a base, usually for a savoury item such as a roast game bird or a meat mixture. Many hors d'œuvres and snacks are served on small round croûtes or fingers of bread. Croûtes are also used as a garnish for a rich dish such as a salmi, their crispness contrasting with the sauce.

Croûtes should be cut from bread at least one day old, and should be $\frac{1}{4}-\frac{1}{2}$ in thick.

To fry croûtes Use clarified butter or oil, and make sure that the first side is crisp and golden before turning.

To make toasted croûtes Toast whole bread slices, and cut to shape after toasting, using a sharp knife or scissors.

To make croûtons Croûtons are small squares or dice of fried or toasted bread served with soups or game, or as a garnish for egg or vegetable dishes. Cut the crusts off $\frac{1}{4}-\frac{1}{2}$ in slices of day-old bread, cut into dice, and fry until golden on all sides. If you prefer, sprinkle the croûtons with melted butter, and bake until golden and crisp.

CUMBERLAND SAUCE

1 orange	$\frac{1}{4}$ teasp mixed
1 lemon	mustard
$\frac{1}{8}$ pt water	Salt
$\frac{1}{8}$ pt port wine	Cayenne pepper
2 tablesp vinegar	
$\frac{1}{4}$ lb redcurrant jelly	

Grate the rind of the orange and lemon, carefully avoiding the pith. Simmer the rinds in the water for 10 min. Add the wine, vinegar, jelly and mustard and simmer them together until the jelly is completely melted. Add the juice of the orange and lemon, season to taste and cool.

ESPAGNOLE SAUCE

1 onion	2 oz butter *or*
1 carrot	dripping
2 oz mushrooms *or* mushroom trimmings	2 oz flour
	1 pt brown stock
	Bouquet garni
2 oz lean raw ham *or* bacon	6 peppercorns
	1 bay leaf

$\frac{1}{4}$ pt tomato pulp	$\frac{1}{8}$ pt sherry
Salt	(optional)

Slice the vegetables, chop the ham. Melt the fat and fry the ham for a few minutes and then, very slowly, the vegetables until they are golden-brown. Add the flour and continue frying very slowly till all is a rich brown. Add the stock, herbs and spices and stir till the sauce simmers; simmer for $\frac{1}{2}$ hr. Add the tomato pulp and simmer the sauce for a further $\frac{1}{2}$ hr. Wring the sauce through a tammy cloth or rub it through a fine hair or nylon sieve. Season, add the sherry, if used, and re-heat the sauce.

For demi-glace sauce, boil together $\frac{1}{2}$ pt Espagnole sauce, $\frac{1}{4}$ pt roast meat juices or stock and 1 teasp meat glaze. Reduce well, and skim off any fat.

FLAKY PASTRY

1 lb flour	Cold water to mix
Pinch of salt	$\frac{1}{2}$ teasp lemon
10 oz butter *or*	juice
butter and lard	

Sift the flour and salt into a basin. Divide the butter into 4 equal pieces and rub $\frac{1}{4}$ of it (1 piece) into the flour. If butter and lard are used, blend them together well before dividing into 4 pieces. Mix to a soft dough with cold water and lemon juice, making it the same consistency as the remaining butter.

Roll out into an oblong strip and flake another $\frac{1}{4}$ piece of the butter on the $\frac{2}{3}$ of the pastry farthest from you. Dredge lightly with flour, fold the uncovered $\frac{1}{3}$ of the pastry over, on to the fat and then fold over it the fat-flaked top $\frac{1}{3}$ of pastry. Press the edges of the pastry 'packet' together lightly with the rolling pin, to prevent butter or air being squeezed out. Half-turn the pastry, so that the folded edges are right and left when rolling. With the rolling pin, press ridges in the pastry to distribute the air evenly. Roll out. Allow the dough to relax in a cool place for 10 min.

Repeat the process twice to incorporate the remaining two $\frac{1}{4}$ pieces of the butter.

Rubbing fat into flour   Putting fat flakes on dough

Put flaky pastry into a very hot oven (230 °C, 450 °F, Gas 8) until set, then reduce heat to 190 °C, 375 °F, Gas 5 for as long as required.

To make Patty Cases Roll out puff or flaky pastry to a thickness of $\frac{1}{8}$ in and cut into rounds with a $2\frac{1}{2}$-in or 3-in cutter. Remove the centres from half of these rounds with a $1\frac{1}{4}$-in or $1\frac{1}{2}$-in cutter. Turn the pastry upside down after cutting. Moisten the plain halves and place the ringed halves evenly on top. Prick the centres. Place on a baking tray and allow to stand for at least 10 min in a cold place. Glaze the ringed halves and the small lids and bake in a very hot oven (230 °C, 450 °F, Gas 8). When baked, remove and scoop out any soft inside part. If liked the cases can be made as vol-au-vent cases.

FRENCH DRESSING

2–3 tablesp olive oil	1 tablesp wine vinegar
Pepper and salt	

Mix the oil and seasoning. Add the vinegar gradually, stirring constantly with a wooden spoon so that an emulsion is formed.

Alternatively, make the sauce in a bottle with a tight stopper. Keep it in the fridge, and shake vigorously before use. French dressing will keep for several days if chilled.

Lemon juice can be used in place of vinegar. Where suitable, orange or grapefruit juice can also be used.

A pinch of sugar, a little mustard and one or two drops of Worcester sauce can be added.

GLAZE FOR MEAT DISHES, OR MEAT GLAZE

Strictly, you should reduce about 4 qt clear stock to about $\frac{1}{4}$ pt by continued boiling, uncovered. It is cheaper and quicker to add enough gelatine to strong stock to set it almost firm.

GRAVY for Game

Bones, giblets _or_ trimmings of game	1 clove 6 peppercorns and 1 piece of
Cold water to cover	onion to each pt of water
1 bay leaf	Salt
Thyme	

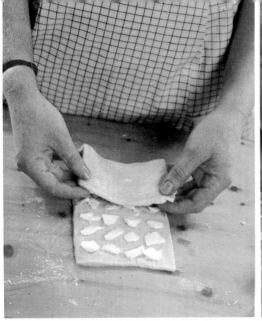

Folding fat-flaked pastry

The folded pastry 'resting'

Make stock from the above ingredients. Drain all the fat from the roasting-tin and rinse the tin with the game stock, using no flour. Boil the gravy and skim it.

GRAVY—for any Roast Joint except Pork

Meat dripping from the roasting tin	Water in which vegetables have been boiled *or* stock
Flour	
Essences from the joint	Salt and pepper

Drain most of the fat from the roasting tin, carefully saving any sediment and meat juices. Dredge into the thin film of dripping sufficient flour to absorb it all. Brown this flour slowly till of a nut-brown colour. Stir in water in which green vegetables or potatoes have been cooked, or stock, allowing $\frac{1}{2}$ pt for 6 persons. Boil the gravy and season it to taste.

To obtain a brown colour without browning the flour, add a few drips of gravy browning from the end of a skewer.

GRAVY (thickened) for a Stuffed Joint or for Roast Pork

Bones and trimmings from the joint	Cold water
	Salt
To each pint of gravy :	
1 oz dripping	1 oz flour

Make a stock from the bones, allowing at least 2 hr simmering—longer if possible.

Melt dripping and sprinkle in the flour. Brown the flour slowly until a nut-brown colour. Stir in the stock, boil up and season to taste.

GREEN SALAD AS GARNISH
See Lettuce Salad

Note that you can use endive for a green salad in the same way as lettuce.

HOLLANDAISE SAUCE

2 tablesp wine vinegar	2–4 oz butter
	Salt and pepper
2 egg yolks	Lemon juice

Boil the vinegar till it is reduced by half; allow to cool. Mix the cool vinegar with the egg yolks in a basin and place this over hot water. Whisk the egg yolks till they begin to thicken, then whisk in the butter gradually until all is absorbed. Season, add lemon juice to taste and serve immediately.

HOT WATER CRUST PASTRY

For Pork, Veal and Ham or Raised Game Pies

10 oz plain flour	**3 oz lard**
½ teasp salt	**¼ pt milk *or* water**

Sift the flour and salt into a warm bowl, make a well in the centre, and keep in a warm place. Heat the lard and milk *or* water together gently until boiling then add them to the flour, mixing well with a wooden spoon, until cool enough to knead with the hands. Knead thoroughly. Leave covered for ½ hr. Then use as required.

Throughout the processes of mixing, kneading and moulding, the pastry must be kept warm. But if it is too warm it will be so soft and pliable that it cannot retain its shape, or support its own weight.

Bake in a hot oven (220 °C, 425 °F, Gas 7), reducing heat to moderate (180 °C, 350 °F, Gas 4) as soon as pastry is set.

To raise a pie The pastry must be raised or moulded whilst still warm. Reserve ¼ for the lid and leave in the bowl in a warm place covered with a cloth. Roll out the remainder to about ¼ in thickness in a round or oval shape. Gently mould the pie with the hands; if this proves too difficult, mould it over an inverted, greased and floured jam jar.

When cold, remove the pastry case from the jar, put in the filling. Roll the ¼ of pastry reserved for the lid, damp the rim of the case, put on the lid and press edges firmly together.

Three or four folds of greased paper should be pinned round the pie to preserve its shape during baking and to prevent it becoming too brown.

Note: If the pie is raised without using a jar, when the lower part of the pie has been raised to the required shape and thinness, moulding can be made easier by pressing in firmly some of the filling to support the lower part of the pie.

JAM SAUCE

4 good tablesp jam	**1 heaped teasp arrowroot**
½ pt water	

Mix and heat gently until thick.

MAÎTRE D'HÔTEL BUTTER

Use 2 oz butter and salt and pepper to taste with these ingredients: 2 teasp finely chopped parsley, ½ teasp each chopped chervil and tarragon (optional), ½ teasp lemon juice. Spread on a plate and chill after making, cut out round pats and use to top fish, steaks, etc.

MAÎTRE D'HÔTEL SAUCE

½ pt basic white sauce	**fine-chopped parsley**
Juice of ½ lemon	**1 oz butter**
1½ tablesp	

Just before serving, combine all the ingredients.

MAYONNAISE

1–2 egg yolks	**Mixed vinegars**
Salt and pepper	**to taste—if**
Mustard	**possible, 4 parts**
¼–½ pt best olive oil	**wine, vinegar *or* lemon juice,**
	2 parts tarragon and 1 part chilli vinegar

The eggs and oil should be at the same temperature and not too cold. In summer it is easier to make a good mayonnaise beginning with 2 egg yolks.

Remove every trace of egg white from the yolks. Put the yolks in a thick basin which will stand steady in spite of vigorous beating. Add to the egg yolks the pepper, salt and mustard to taste. Drop by drop, add the olive oil, beating or whisking vigorously all the time. As the mayonnaise thickens, the olive oil can be poured in a thin, steady stream but whisking must never slacken. When the mixture is really thick a few drops of vinegar or lemon juice stirred in will thin it again. Continue whisking in the oil, alternately with a little vinegar until the whole amount is added.

If the mayonnaise should curdle, break a fresh egg yolk into a clean basin and beat into this the curdled mixture just as the oil was added originally.

Various other ingredients are often added to mayonnaise, to give a different flavour and colour. They are useful when making a mixed hors d'œuvre or any other dish of mixed products coated with mayonnaise, for they identify the different ingredients, and emphasize their variety.

Some variations are complex sauces in their own right. But it is hardly worth making these for light savoury dishes where, as a rule, only a small amount of each sauce is needed. So the following simple additions to plain Mayonnaise are suggested instead.

To ¼ pt mayonnaise, add:

1 2 tablesp concentrated tomato purée and 1 sweet red pepper, chopped (Andalusian Sauce)

2 1 tablesp cooked spinach purée and 2 tablesp single cream (Green Mousseline Sauce)

3 ½ teasp horseradish cream, 1 teasp each chopped parsley and chervil (Escoffier Sauce)

4 1 tablesp yogurt (or sour cream), ½ teasp chopped chives and a few drops each of Worcester Sauce and lemon juice (Gloucester Sauce)

5 1 oz mixed chopped fresh herbs, as many as you can get (Green Mayonnaise)

An electric blender makes almost foolproof mayonnaise. Use a whole egg instead of yolks and 2 tablesp vinegar. Put these into the goblet with the seasoning and whisk at high speed for 10 seconds. Still whisking, trickle in the oil gradually. The mixture will start to thicken after ¼ pt has gone in, and will not 'take' more than ½ pt.

White wine can be used instead of wine vinegar, and wine vinegar with a drop or two of Tabasco Sauce can replace the chilli vinegar.

MINT SAUCE

3 heaped tablesp finely chopped mint	2 teasp sugar
A pinch of salt	2 tablesp boiling water
	¼ pt vinegar

The mint should be young and freshly gathered if possible. Wash well, pick the leaves from the stalks and chop the leaves finely.

Mix the mint, salt and sugar in the sauceboat. Pour on to them the boiling water and leave the mixture to cool. Add the vinegar and if possible leave the sauce for 1 hr to infuse the flavour of mint into the vinegar. Serve with roast lamb.

MUSHROOM SAUCE (BROWN)

| ½ pt basic brown sauce |
| 2–4 oz mushrooms (field if possible) |

Chop the mushroom stalks and fry with the other vegetables when making the brown sauce. Add the mushrooms with the stock when making the sauce, and simmer until tender. Strain the sauce, chop the mushrooms and return them to the sauce.

ORANGE SALAD

Allow the oranges to stand in boiling water for a few minutes, peel them and remove all pith. Cut fruit into thin slices, removing pips. Sprinkle slices with a little sugar and French dressing, to which a little brandy may be added if liked. Garnish with parsley.

3 helpings

PIQUANT SAUCE

½ pt basic brown sauce	1 tablesp halved capers
1 onion or 2 shallots	1 tablesp chopped gherkins
1 oz mushrooms	1 dessertsp mushroom ketchup
1 bay leaf	
¼ teasp mace	½ teasp sugar (optional)
2 tablesp vinegar	

Finely chop the onion or shallots and chop the mushrooms coarsely. Simmer the onion or shallots, the bay leaf and mace in the vinegar for 10 min. Add this mixture and the chopped mushrooms to the brown sauce and simmer till the mushrooms are soft. Add all the other ingredients. Do not strain the sauce but lift out the bay leaf and mace. Serve with pork, mutton or vegetables.

PRAWN OR SHRIMP SAUCE

To $\frac{1}{2}$ pt white stock made with $\frac{1}{2}$ fish stock and $\frac{1}{4}$ milk, add $\frac{1}{4}$ pt cooked shelled prawns (fresh or frozen), a few drops of anchovy essence and lemon juice to taste. Colour very lightly with a drop or two of pink colouring. Season with a little cayenne pepper, and re-heat very gently without boiling.

PUFF PASTRY

For Tartlets, Patties, Vols-au-Vent, etc

1 lb butter	2 egg yolks
1 lb plain flour	$\frac{1}{3}$ pt cold water
$\frac{1}{2}$ teasp salt	(approx)

Squeeze the butter in a floured cloth to remove as much moisture as possible. Put 2 oz aside and form the remainder into a flat cake. Keep in a cool place. Sift the flour and salt and rub in the 2 oz butter. Mix to a firm dough with the egg yolks and water, and knead quickly and lightly till smooth. Roll out into an oblong about $\frac{1}{2}$ in thick, keeping the ends square, and enfold the cake of butter in the pastry. Press lightly with the rolling-pin until the butter is flattened. Roll out into a strip as thinly as possible without allowing the butter to break through, fold in three, seal the edges using the rolling-pin, and put aside in a cool place for about 15 min to allow the pastry to become sufficiently cool and firm. Roll and fold it twice, half turning the pastry between each rolling and leave in a cool place again for 15 min. After the pastry has been rolled and folded seven times it is ready for use.

To make a Vol-au-Vent case Roll out the puff pastry to about $\frac{3}{4}$-in thickness, and

with a cutter previously dipped in flour, cut into a round or oval shape as desired. Cut cleanly without dragging or twisting the pastry. Place on a baking-sheet, brush over the top of the pastry with beaten egg. With a smaller, floured cutter cut an inner ring, cutting the pastry to about $\frac{1}{2}$ its depth. Bake in a very hot oven (230 °C, 450 °F, Gas 8). When baked, remove the lid and scoop out the soft inside.

RISOTTO

4 oz long-grain rice	Salt and pepper
1 small onion	2 tablesp grated Parmesan cheese
2 oz butter	
1 pt vegetable stock or water	

Wash and dry the rice thoroughly. Chop the onion finely; heat the butter and fry the onion until lightly browned. Then add the rice and fry it until brown. Put in the stock or water, add salt and pepper to taste, boil rapidly for 10 min and afterwards simmer slowly until the rice has absorbed all the liquid. Stir in the cheese, add more seasoning if necessary, then serve.

This savoury rice is frequently used for borders instead of plainly boiled rice or mashed potatoes.

ROUGH PUFF PASTRY

$\frac{1}{2}$ lb plain flour	$\frac{1}{2}$ teasp lemon juice
Pinch of salt	
6 oz butter or butter and lard	Cold water to mix

Sift the flour and salt. Add the butter cut up into pieces the size of a walnut and mix lightly with the flour. Make a well in the centre, put in the lemon juice and gradually add sufficient water to mix to an elastic dough. Roll into a long strip, keeping the corners square, fold into three. With the rolling-pin seal the edges and give the pastry a half-turn, so that the folded edges are on the right and left. Repeat until the pastry has been rolled and folded 4 times, if possible leaving for 15 min in a cool place between the second and third rollings.

Use as required. Bake in a very hot oven (230 °C, 450 °F, Gas 8).

SAGE AND ONION STUFFING

$\frac{1}{4}$ lb onions	2 oz breadcrumbs
4 sage leaves *or*	1 oz butter
$\frac{1}{2}$ teasp	Salt and pepper
powdered sage	1 egg (optional)

Slice the onions thickly, parboil them for 10 min in very little water. Scald the sage leaves. Chop both. Mash all the ingredients together and season to your taste.

SAUSAGE MEAT STUFFING

$\frac{1}{2}$ lb lean pork	Grated nutmeg
2 oz breadcrumbs	to taste
$\frac{1}{2}$ teasp mixed	The liver of the
fresh herbs *or*	bird to be stuffed
$\frac{1}{4}$ teasp dried	Stock
herbs	
2 small sage	
leaves	
Salt and pepper	

Mince the pork. Chop the liver. Mix all the ingredients, using enough stock to bind the mixture. Season to taste.

Use for turkey or chicken.

A good bought pork sausage meat mixed with the liver of the bird makes a quick stuffing for poultry.

SHERRY OR WINE SAUCE, SWEET

$\frac{1}{8}$ pt water
$\frac{1}{8}$ pt sherry *or*
sweet white wine
2 tablesp any
jam *or* jelly
Sugar to taste
Lemon juice to
taste

Simmer all the ingredients together for 5 min. Rub through a hair or nylon sieve or strain the sauce. Adjust the flavour, re-heat if necessary. If you wish, this sauce can be thickened like Jam Sauce.

SHORT CRUST PASTRY, ALL-PURPOSE

$\frac{1}{2}$ lb plain flour	2 oz lard
Pinch of salt	Cold water
2 oz butter	

Sift the flour and salt. Rub in the fat, add baking powder and using a knife, mix to a stiff dough with cold water. Use as required.

Bake in a very hot oven (230 °C, 450 °F, Gas 8), until set, and lower the heat later to cook filling.

For savoury tarts, a little spice or a few finely chopped herbs can be added.

For Rich Short Crust Pastry

$\frac{1}{2}$ lb plain flour	1 egg yolk
4-6 oz butter	Cold water to
(sweet cream	mix (about
type, if possible)	1 tablesp)
1 teasp castor	
sugar	

Make as above, on a flat surface rather than in a bowl. Before adding water, make a well in the dry ingredients, and put in the egg yolk. Sprinkle with the sugar, and mix with the finger-tips or a knife. Add the water as required, and mix.

BROWN STOCK MADE WITH MEAT FOR CLEAR GRAVIES, ETC

At least 2 lb veal	Salt and pepper
and beef bones,	1 carrot
mixed	1 stick of celery
1-2 lb shin beef	1 onion
(lean only)	Bouquet garni
3 qt cold water	

Scrape the bones, remove every scrap of fat and marrow and wash well in hot water. Wipe the meat with a damp cloth and cut it into small pieces, after removing any fat. Put all the bones and meat into a pan and add the cold water and seasoning. Soak for $\frac{1}{2}$ hr. Bring very slowly to simmering point and simmer for 1 hr. Add the vegetables whole, including a piece of outer brown skin of onion and the bouquet garni, and simmer for a further 3 hr. Strain the stock through a metal sieve.

To clear the stock, beat 3 egg whites until frothy. Put into a pan with the strained stock, and simmer very gently for 1 hr. Strain slowly through a finely woven cotton cloth.

If jellied stock is wanted, 2 oz dissolved gelatine can be added to the stock and well stirred in before cooking. For a rich stock, reduce to the strength required by simmering, uncovered.

STOCK FOR GENERAL USE

Cooked *or* raw bones of any kind of meat	1 outside stick of celery
Cooked or raw skin, gristle and trimmings of lean meat	1 onion 1 bay leaf Peppercorns
Clean peelings of carrots, turnip, mushrooms	
Salt	

Break or chop the bones to 3-in pieces and put them with the skin and trimmings into a strong pan. Cover with cold water and add $\frac{1}{2}$ teasp salt to each quart of water. Bring slowly to simmering point. Add the vegetables, including a piece of outer brown skin of onion, if a brown stock is required. Simmer for at least 3 hr, without a lid on top heat, or covered in a slow oven. Bones may be cooked until they are porous and so soft that they crumble when crushed, but they should be strained and cooled at the end of each day, the vegetables removed at once, and fresh water added next day. If the stock is not required at once it must be cooled quickly, kept cold—preferably in a fridge—and used within 24 hr even in cool weather or within 3 days if kept in a fridge.

Before use, skim the fat from the top of the stock. This may be clarified with other meat fat, or used as needed in meat cookery.

Quantity—1$\frac{1}{2}$ pt from each 1 lb bones, etc.

FISH STOCK

Bones, skin and heads from fish which have been filleted *or* fish trimmings *or* cods' or other fish heads	Peppercorns 1 onion 1 stick of celery $\frac{1}{4}$ teasp mace 1 bay leaf Bouquet garni
Salt	

Wash the fish trimmings and break up the bones. Cover them with cold water, add salt and bring slowly to simmering point. Add the other ingredients and simmer gently for no longer than 40 min. If cooked for longer the fish stock will taste bitter. Strain and use the same day if possible. Fish stock does not keep and should be made as required.

POULTRY OR GAME STOCK

Carcass of chicken, duck *or* game bird, with giblets if available Cleaned feet of bird	Giblets Salt Cold water to cover 1 onion White peppercorns

Make like Brown Stock, Made with Meat.

STOCK FOR CONSOMMÉ, ETC

2–3 lb veal and beef bones mixed (for brown stock) *or* veal and chicken bones (for white stock) 3 qt cold water Small strip lemon rind (white stock only)	1$\frac{1}{2}$ teasp salt 1 carrot (brown stock only) 1 onion (peeled for white stock) 1 stick celery *or* 1 leek 6 peppercorns 1 bay leaf

Scrape the bones if required, and wash them. Put into a pan and add the water and salt. Soak for 1 hr. Bring very slowly to simmering point, and simmer for 1 hr. Add the vegetables, whole, and the remaining ingredients. Simmer for 3–4 hr. Strain and use.

TO 'CLEAR' STOCK FOR CONSOMMÉ (AND FOR ASPIC JELLY, ETC)

1 qt clear stock, free from fat	$\frac{1}{4}$ pt water
1 small onion, peeled and parboiled	2 tablesp sherry
	1 egg white
1 small carrot, scraped	$\frac{1}{4}$ teasp salt and pepper mixed
1 small stick celery	Small pinch nutmeg *or* mace
$\frac{1}{4}$ lb lean shin of beef *or* skirt	

Scrub the vegetables and chop roughly. Chop or mince the beef finely and soak it for $\frac{1}{4}$ hr in the cold water. Beat the egg white until stiff. Put all the ingredients into a pan and bring them slowly to simmering point. Simmer very gently without touching the pan for 1 hr. Strain very carefully through a woollen or cotton cloth.

VEGETABLE STOCK AND GRAVY

2 large carrots	Bouquet garni
$\frac{1}{2}$ lb onions	1 teasp salt
3 sticks celery	$\frac{1}{2}$ teasp peppercorns
2 tomatoes	
$\frac{1}{4}$ small cabbage	Pinch of ground mace
1 oz butter *or* margarine	1 bay leaf
2 qt boiling water	
$\frac{1}{2}$ teasp vegetable extract	

Wash, peel and cut up the vegetables. Fry the roots gently in the fat until golden-brown. Add the tomatoes and fry a little. Add all the other ingredients except the cabbage and simmer for 1 hr. Add the cabbage and simmer another 20 min. Strain and use as soon as possible.

For gravy use 1 pt of this stock with 1 tablesp mushroom ketchup and 1 teasp walnut ketchup (optional). Mix the ketchups

smoothly with 1 teasp arrowroot, and browning if desired. Add a few drops of sherry (optional). Stir the arrowroot mixture into the stock, bring to simmering point and stir. Simmer until the desired consistency and flavour is reached.

WHITE STOCK

2 lb knuckle of veal	Small strip of lemon rind
2 qt cold water	1 bay leaf
1 teasp salt	
1 dessertsp white vinegar *or* lemon juice	
1 onion	
1 stick of celery	
$\frac{1}{2}$ teasp white peppercorns	

Make like Brown Stock, Made with Meat.

Quantity about 3 pt

SUET CRUST PASTRY

For Meat puddings, Fruit puddings, Jam Roly Poly, Suet Puddings, etc.

3–4 oz suet
$\frac{1}{2}$ lb plain flour
$\frac{1}{4}$ teasp salt
1 teasp baking powder
Cold water to mix

Chop the suet finely with a little flour or use shredded suet. Sift the flour, salt and baking powder, and mix in the suet. Mix to a firm dough with cold water.

SUET DUMPLINGS

3–4 oz suet
$\frac{1}{2}$ lb flour
$\frac{1}{4}$ teasp salt
1 teasp baking powder
Cold water

Make like suet crust pastry; form into small balls and drop into boiling stock; after 3 min reduce heat and simmer for 15–20 min.

SUPRÊME SAUCE

$\frac{1}{2}$ pt Velouté sauce	Nutmeg to
2 tablesp—$\frac{1}{8}$ pt	taste
cream	Lemon juice
1 egg yolk	Salt and pepper
$\frac{1}{2}$–1 oz butter	

Heat the Velouté sauce, preferably in a double boiler. Mix the egg yolk and cream, and stir into the sauce. Cook without boiling until the egg yolk thickens. Whisk in the butter, a small pat at a time. Add a pinch of nutmeg, a few drops of lemon juice, season and use the sauce at once.

TOMATO SAUCE

1 onion	$\frac{1}{2}$ pt white stock
1 small carrot	or liquid from
1 oz bacon	canned or bottled
scraps or bacon	tomatoes
bone or rinds	Salt and pepper
$\frac{1}{2}$ oz butter or	Lemon juice
margarine	Sugar
4 medium-sized	Grated nutmeg
tomatoes, fresh,	
bottled or canned	
$\frac{1}{2}$ oz cornflour	

Slice the onion and carrot. Put them into a saucepan with the bacon and fry them in the fat without browning them for 10 min. Slice and add the tomatoes and cook them for 5 min. Sprinkle in the cornflour, add the stock or juice, stir till the sauce boils. Simmer the sauce for 45 min. Rub the sauce through a hair or nylon sieve. Re-heat, season and add lemon juice, sugar and nutmeg to taste.

VEAL FORCEMEAT OR FORCEMEAT BALLS

4 oz breadcrumbs	Nutmeg
2 oz chopped suet	Grated rind of $\frac{1}{2}$
or margarine	lemon
1 tablesp chopped	Salt and pepper
parsley	1 beaten egg
$\frac{1}{2}$ teasp chopped	
mixed herbs	

Mix all the ingredients well together, using the egg to form a stiff paste. If liked, roll into balls and fry in deep or shallow fat until golden-brown all over.

VELOUTÉ SAUCE

2 oz butter	2 oz flour
6 button mush-	1 pt good
rooms or mush-	vegetable stock
room trimmings	Salt and pepper
12 peppercorns	Lemon juice
A few parsley	$\frac{1}{8}$–$\frac{1}{4}$ pt cream
stalks	

Melt the butter in a saucepan and cook the mushrooms, peppercorns and parsley gently for 10 min. Add the flour and cook for a few minutes without browning it. Stir in the stock, bring the sauce to simmering point and simmer for 1 hr. Wring the sauce through damp muslin. Season, add lemon juice, and re-heat. Just at boiling point stir in the cream. The mushrooms may be rinsed and used as garnish for the dish. For fish dishes, use fish stock.

VINAIGRETTE SAUCE

This consists of a simple French dressing to which the following are added:

1 teasp finely chopped gherkin
$\frac{1}{2}$ teasp finely chopped shallot or chives
$\frac{1}{2}$ teasp finely chopped parsley
1 teasp finely chopped capers
$\frac{1}{2}$ teasp finely chopped tarragon and chervil (if available)

WHITE WINE SAUCE (SAVOURY)

$\frac{1}{2}$ pt white stock or	$\frac{1}{8}$ pt white wine
fish stock	1–2 egg yolks
2 oz butter	Juice of $\frac{1}{2}$ lemon
1 oz flour	Salt and pepper

Make a white sauce with the stock, $\frac{1}{2}$ the butter and the flour. Add the wine to this and simmer it for 10 min. Whisk in the remaining butter just below boiling point, then stir in the egg yolks mixed with lemon juice; season. Thicken the egg yolks without letting the sauce boil again.

top left: Carrots cooked for food value

top right: Dressed crab

right: Apple fritters

Menus

All the named dishes are given in this book.
All the other items are described in
Mrs Beeton's Cookery and Household Management.

FAMILY BREAKFAST I
Fresh Orange Juice
Scrambled Eggs on Toasted Croûtes
Toast, butter and marmalade
Tea or Coffee

FAMILY BREAKFAST II
Fresh Fruit (e.g. grapefruit)
Baked Eggs—Coquette Style
Toast, butter and honey
Tea or Coffee

ONE MAN'S (OR WOMAN'S) BREAKFAST
Fresh Fruit (e.g. $\frac{1}{2}$ grapefruit)
English Omelet or Poached Egg on
Toasted Croûte
Tea or Coffee

SUNDAY BRUNCH I
Savoury Pancakes
Grilled Bacon
Large Sausages
Devilled Butter Sandwiches
Fresh Fruit
Coffee

SUNDAY BRUNCH II
Toasted Sandwiches
with Bacon and Mushroom Filling
Apples Filled with Banana and Nut Salad
Coffee

SMALL CHILDREN'S LUNCH
French Omelettes aux fines herbes
Creamed Potatoes
Baked Apples and Cream
Milk

SCHOOL PACKED LUNCH
2 Two-Decker Sandwiches *or*
Scotch Egg
Fresh Fruit

FAMILY'S SUNDAY DINNER
Roast Chicken with Bread Sauce
Potato Chips
Brussels Sprouts with Chestnuts
Gravy   Redcurrant Jelly
Apple or other Fruit Crumble
with Cream
Coffee

FAMILY DINNER (EVENING) I
Beef Broth with Golden Roll Slices
Grilled Mackerel with Gooseberry Sauce
Mashed Potatoes
Boiled French *or* Runner Beans
Pancakes
Coffee

FAMILY DINNER (EVENING) II
Tomato Soup
Braised Pork Chops in Cider
Boiled Haricot Beans
Red Cabbage with Apples
Basic Milanaise Soufflé
Coffee

FORMAL DINNER (EVENING) I
Consommé Royale with Royale
Custard Shapes
Braised Duck with Chestnuts or Fruit
Sautéed Potatoes
Lettuce Salad
Meringue Gâteau
Coffee

FORMAL DINNER (EVENING) II
Cold Cheese Soufflé
Escalopes of Veal, Viennese Style
Potato Straws
Cucumber Salad
Peach Melba
Coffee

ONE MAN'S (OR WOMAN'S) SUPPER
Smoked Fish and brown bread and butter
Sautéed Kidneys
Fried or Grilled Tomatoes
Potato Salad
Fresh Fruit
Coffee

SUNDAY EVENING SUPPER (FAMILY)
Minestrone
Savoury Stuffed Ham Rolls
Veal and Ham Pie
Baked Potatoes in their Jackets
Basic Vanilla Ice Cream
Tea or Coffee

T.V. OR TRAY SUPPER (FAMILY) I
Liver Pâté and Toast
Cumberland Lamb or Mutton Pies
Fresh Tomatoes
Fruit Flan or Tart
Coffee *or* Milk with Ice Cream

T.V. OR TRAY SUPPER (FAMILY) II
Cheese Flan
Baked Stuffed Potatoes
with Smoked Haddock Filling
Carrot Salad
Meringues
Tea or Coffee

Potatoes baked in their jackets
far right: Apple pie

below right: French onion soup
below: Apple charlotte

Index

Anchovy butter 108
Anchovy sauce 108
Apple charlotte 102
Apple dumplings 102
Apple or other fruit
crumble 102
Apple pie 103
Apple sauce 108
Apples, banana and nut
salad 91
Asparagus au naturel 14
Aspic jelly 1 108
Aspic jelly 2 109
Avocado pears and
prawns 15

Bacon with fruit 66
Baked apples 102
Baked eggs 19
Baked frozen haddock fillets
with cucumber sauce 30
Baked haddock and
orange 30
Baked ham 47
Baked onions 87
Baked or steamed
custard 95
Baked ox liver 62
Baked tomatoes 89
Banana split 107
Basic brown sauce 109
Basic ice cream
(vanilla) 106

Basic ice cream
custards 106
Basic Milanaise soufflé 104
Basic white sauce 109
Batter pudding, baked or
steamed 97
Béchamel sauce 109
Beef, lamb or mutton
hash 57
Beef olives 50
Beetroot salad 91
Blanquette of lamb or
veal 56
Beurre manié 110
Boiled or baked corn on
the cob 90
Boiled beef, fresh or
salted 53
Boiled brussels sprouts with
chestnuts 84
Boiled cabbage 84
Boiled cauliflower with
white sauce 86
Boiled fowl with
oysters 72
Boiled French or runner
beans 83
Boiled ham or bacon 55
Boiled leg of lamb or
mutton 54
Boiled lentils 86
Boiled, mashed or
creamed potatoes 88

Boiled pickled pork or
bacon with beans 55
Boiled or poached salmon
and salmon trout 31
Boiled rice 110
Boiled tongue 63
Bouquet garni (bunch of
fresh herbs) 110
Brandy butter 110
Braised beef in aspic 63

Braised beef with
peppers 50
Braised celery 86
Braised duck with
chestnuts and fruit 72
Braised leg or shoulder
of lamb 50
Braised pork chops in
cider 51
Braised sweetbreads 63
Braised turkey or
chicken 71
Bread and butter
pudding 96
Bread sauce 110
Broad beans with parsley
sauce 84
Brown sauce, basic 109
Brown stock for clear
gravies, etc 117
Burnt almond ice
cream 106

Capkin or mixed fish grill 34
Carrots—cooked for food value 86
Carrot salad 91
Casseroled lambs' hearts 61
Cauliflower with cheese 89
Châteaubriand steak 44
Cheese fondue 20
Chequerboard salad 35
Chicken à la Minute 68
Chicken 'en casserole' 70
Chicken Marengo 70
Chicken pie 74
Chicken pilaff 71
Chicken salad 74
Chicken with supréme sauce 73
Chicken vol-au-vent 74
Chocolate soufflé 97
Christmas pudding (economical, boiled or steamed) 99
Christmas pudding (rich, boiled) 98
Clearing stock for consommé 119
Compote of pigeons or partridges 78
Consommé (basic) 10
Consommé Julienne 10
Consommé Royale 10
Corned beef pie 59
Court bouillon 110
Crab salad 39
Creamed scampi 42
Croûtes and croûtons 111
Crown roast of lamb with saffron rice 44
Cucumber salad 91
Cumberland sauce 111
Curried chicken or turkey 71
Curried crab 38
Custards and custard mixtures 95

Devilled turkey legs 70
Dressed crab in shell 38
Dressed lobster 40
Duck salad 75

Eggs in aspic 16
Eggs à la Dijon 14
English omelet 19
Escalopes of veal, Viennese style 47
Espagnole sauce 111
Exeter stew 54

Fillets of plaice with lemon dressing 35
Fillets of sole bonne femme 32
Fish cakes 34
Fish stock 118
Flaky pastry 111
Flavourings for milk and custard puddings 95
French dressing 112
French omelette 19
French onion soup 10
Fricassée of cooked chicken 73
Fricassée of rabbit 82
Fried artichoke bottoms in batter 83
Fried eggs 18
Fried or grilled tomatoes 89
Fruit flan or tart 103
Fruit pudding with suet crust 99
Fruit purées 106
Fruit salad 106
Frying and grilling bacon 18

'Gefilte' Fish 36
Goulash of beef 54
Gravy for game 112
Gravy for any Roast joint except pork 113
Gravy (thickened) 113
Green peas 87
Green salad as garnish: see lettuce salad
Grilled chicken with mushroom sauce 70
Grilled herrings with mustard sauce 35
Grilled kidneys 62
Grilled lamb or pork cutlets or chops 46
Grilled mackerel with gooseberry sauce 34

Grilled mushrooms 87
Grilled salmon 35
Grilled steak 44

Hamburgers 22
Haricot mutton 55
Hawaiian Dreams 107
Hollandaise sauce 113
Hors D'Oeuvres 13
Hot savoury toasts 22
Hot soufflés (sweet) 96
Hot vol-au-vent or toasted sandwich fillings 28
Hot water crust pastry 79, 114

Irish stew 55
Italian bavarois or cream 104

Jam sauce 114
Jugged and grilled kippers 34
Jugged hare 81
Jugged pigeons 78

Kedgeree 33

Lancashire hot pot 51
Large grain milk puddings 94
Large grain milk puddings with eggs 94
Lemon meringue pie 103
Lemon pudding 99
Lemon water ice 107
Lettuce salad 91
Liver pâté 16
Lobster thermidor 39
Loin of veal, daube style 53

Macaroni au gratin with bacon rolls 22
Maitre D'Hotel butter 114
Maitre D'Hotel sauce 114
Mayonnaise 114
Medium and small grain milk puddings 94
Medium and small grain milk puddings with eggs 95
Melba sauce 107
Meringue topping with shells 105
Minestrone 11

Mint sauce 115
Mushroom sauce
(brown) 115
Mutton or lamb
kebabs 46

Navarin of lamb 51

Omelet fillings 19
Omelets, Omelettes 19
Open sandwiches 26
Orange salad 115
Oxtail stew 62
Oysters au naturel 15
Oysters and their
preparation. 42

Pancakes 98
Pastry cases 28
Peach melba 107
Pigeon pie 79
Piquant sauce 115
Plaice mornay 32
Poached cod à la
provencale 31
Poached eggs 18
Poached halibut or turbot
steaks with prawn sauce 31
Poached salmon or salmon
trout served cold 36
Pork pie 66
Pork and onion
dumpling 59
Pot pie or veal 59
Potato chips 88
Potato salad 91
Potato straws 88
Potatoes baked in their
jackets 87
Potatoes, boiled, creamed
or mashed 88
Poultry or game stock 118
Poultry hot-pot 73
Prawn or shrimp
cocktail 15
Prawn or shrimp
sauce 116
Prawns, shrimps and
scampi 42
Preparing and cooking
crawfish and crayfish 39
Preparing scallops 42
Pressed beef 63
Puff pastry 116

Queen of puddings 96
Rabbit pie 82
Rabbit stew—rich 82
Raised game pie 79
Rechauffé of lamb 57
Red cabbage with
apples 85
Rich short crust
pastry 117
Risotto 116
Roast beef 43
Roast chicken 67
Roast duck with apple
sauce or orange
garnish 67
Roast goose 68
Roast grouse or
partridge 75
Roast guinea fowl 70
Roast haunch of
venison 79
Roast leg of lamb 46
Roast pheasant 75
Roast potatoes 88
Roast turkey with
chestnuts 68
Roast wild duck 75
Rough puff pastry 116
Royale custard shapes 10

**Sage and onion
stuffing** 117
Salmi of pheasant 78
Salmon mousse with
aspic 37
Sandwich fillings 24/25
Sandwiches 23
Sausage meat stuffing 117
Sausage rolls 29
Sausages (cocktail,
Frankfurter and
large) 22
Sautéed kidneys 62
Sautéed or tossed
potatoes 89
Savoury batter 21
Savoury pancakes 21
Scalloped crab 38
Scrambled eggs 18
Steak or steak and kidney
pie 58
Steak or steak and kidney
pudding 58
Steamed whiting 33

Stewed venison 81
Stock for consommé,
etc 118
Stock for general use 118
Stuffed peppers 90
Shepherd's pie 58
Sherry or wine sauce
(sweet) 117
Short crust pastry
(all-purpose) 117
Smoked fish 15
Smoked haddock 33
Sole or plaice aux fines
herbes 31
Sole à la portugaise 30
Spiced grapefruit 14
Steamed custard 95
Suet crust pastry 119
Suet dumplings 119
Suprème sauce 120
Sweet fritter coating
batters 98
Syrup for water ices 107

Toad in the hole 58
Toasted sandwiches 27
Tomato salad 92
Tomato sauce 120
Tomato soup 11
Treacle layer pudding 100
Trifle (traditional) 104
Tripe and onions 63
Trout meunière 35
Two-decker sandwiches 27

Veal and ham pie 66
Veal forcemeat or
forcemeat balls 120
Vegetable marrow—
cooked for food value 87
Vegetable pie 90
Vegetable purées and
cream soups 11
Vegetable stock and
gravy 119
Velouté sauce 120
Vinaigrette sauce 120

Welsh rarebit 20
White sauce, basic 109
White stock 119
White wine sauce 120

**Yorkshire or batter
pudding** 43